BUSINESS MANAGEMENT

James L. Burrow

SOUTH-WESTERN
™
THOMSON LEARNING

Australia • Canada • Mexico • Singapore • Spain • United Kingdom • United States

SOUTH-WESTERN
™
THOMSON LEARNING

Business 2000
Business Management
by James L. Burrow

Executive Editor
Eve Lewis

Project Manager
Enid Nagel

Production Manager
Patricia Matthews Boies

Marketing Manager
Nancy A. Long

Marketing Coordinator
Yvonne Patton-Beard

Editor
Colleen A. Farmer

Print Buyer
Kevin L. Kluck

Cover and Internal Design
Bill Spencer

Editorial Assistant
Stephanie L. White

Compositor
New England Typographic Service

Printer
Courier, Kendalville, Inc.

About the Author
James L. Burrow Ph.D., is the coordinator of the graduate Training and Development Program at North Carolina State University in Raleigh, North Carolina. He has been a faculty member at the community college and university levels in marketing and human resources development as well as a consultant to business and public organizations.

For permission to use material from this text or product, contact us by

Tel: 800-730-2214
Fax: 800-730-2215
Web: www.thomsonrights.com

For more information, contact South-Western Educational Publishing, 5101 Madison Road, Cincinnati, OH, 45227-1490. Or you can visit our Internet site at

www.swep.com

International Divisions List

Asia (including India)
Thomson Learning
60 Albert Street, #15-01
Albert Complex
Singapore 189969
Tel 65 336-6411
Fax 65 336-7411

Australia/New Zealand
Nelson
102 Dobbs Street
South Melbourne
Victoria 3205
Australia
Tel 61 (0)3 9685-4111
Fax 61 (0)3 9685-4199

Canada
Nelson
1120 Birchmount Road
Toronto, Ontario
Canada M1K 5G4
Tel (416) 752-9100
Fax (416) 752-8102

Latin America
Thomson Learning
Seneca 53
Colonia Polanco
11560 Mexico, D.F. Mexico
Tel (525) 281-2906
Fax (525) 281-2656

Spain (including Portugal)
Paraninfo
Calle Magallanes 25
28015 Madrid
Espana
Tel 34 (0)91 446-3350
Fax 34 (0)91 445-6218

UK/Europe/Middle East/Africa
Thomson Learning
Berkshire House
168-173 High Holborn
London WC 1V 7AA
United Kingdom
Tel 44 (0)20 497-1422
Fax 44 (0)20 497-1426

HOW TO USE THIS BOOK
ENGAGE STUDENT INTEREST

CAREERS IN BUSINESS
Highlights a real-world company and how it uses advertising.

CAREERS IN BUSINESS
U.S. SMALL BUSINESS ADMINISTRATION

Since 1953, the Small Business Administration (SBA) has provided support to people who start new businesses. Through local offices in every state, the SBA provides free counseling, education, planning tools and materials, and financial assistance.

The SBA manages federal programs that assist women and minority owned businesses to gain government contracts. The SBA also offers programs to help small business owners qualify for loans and other types of financing.

Business Advisors offer counseling and training for new business owners. They also help prepare business plans and develop financial records. To be a Business Advisor, you need several years of experience operating and managing a business. Experienced advisors may not have a college degree, but younger advisors usually have a bachelor's or master's degree in business or a related area.

THINK CRITICALLY
1. Why does the U.S. government want to help small businesses succeed?
2. Do you think business education or business experience is more important for a Business Advisor? Why?

CHAPTER 5
FINANCIAL MANAGEMENT
LESSONS

5.1 FINANCE A BUSINESS

5.2 FINANCIAL SERVICES

5.3 FINANCIAL RECORDS

5.4 CREDIT AND INSURANCE

LESSONS
Make the text easy to use in all classroom environments.

VIDEO
Contains clips from several resources that can be used to introduce concepts in each chapter.

VIDEO
The Chapter 5 video for this module introduces the concepts in this chapter.

PROJECT
Achieve Financial Success

PROJECT OBJECTIVES
- Describe how to finance a new business
- Identify the financial services needed to operate a business
- Understand why financial records are needed in a business
- Protect a business with effective credit plans and insurance

GETTING STARTED
Read through the Project Process below. Make a list of any materials you will need. Decide how you will obtain the needed materials or information.
- Gather information that describes business services offered by banks from the Internet or by contacting a local bank.

PROJECT PROCESS
Part 1 LESSON 1.1 Identify at least three sources of financing available to a new small business and describe the advantages and disadvantages of each.

Part 2 LESSON 1.2 In small groups identify services that banks and other financial institutions offer to businesses. Agree on those most important and least important to the financial success of a new business.

Part 3 LESSON 1.3 Use the Internet to find information on an accounting software package designed for small businesses. Then make a list of the types of financial records that can be maintained using the software.

Part 4 LESSON 1.4 In your groups, write three policies a small business should have when granting credit to customers or using credit to finance business purchases or operations.

CHAPTER REVIEW
Project Wrap-up Discuss in class the mistakes new businesses make that result in financial problems and what owners can do to achieve financial success.

PROJECT
Group or individual activity that has activities for each lesson.

GOALS
Begin each lesson and offer an overview.

CHAPTER 5 **FINANCIAL MANAGEMENT**

LESSON 5.1
FINANCE A BUSINESS

GOALS

RECOGNIZE the ways businesses are financed

DESCRIBE factors to consider in financing business operations

HOW TO FINANCE A BUSINESS

The financial strength of a business is one of the most important factors in its success. Poor financial management is one of the primary reasons businesses fail. Business owners need to have adequate resources to finance business operations and must be effective financial managers to use those resources effectively. **Capital** refers to the financial resources used to operate a business. There are several sources of capital for a business. Each source has advantages and disadvantages.

A business needs money to purchase or rent buildings, obtain equipment, raw materials, and supplies needed to operate the business, hire employees, and pay for the day-to-day operating expenses. That money comes from one of two sources. Financial resources the owners of a business provide is **equity capital**. Money obtained from sources other than business owners is **debt capital**. Debt capital is obtained when a business borrows money or obtains credit to purchase products or services.

ON THE SCENE

Arturo's computer repair business has been open almost two years and he has done quite well. However, he now needs to invest in new equipment that might cost as much as $50,000. Arturo is not quite sure how to obtain the money. He could find a partner to invest in the business or try to obtain a loan from a bank. The loan would result in high interest payments for several years. Are there other ways Arturo can obtain the needed money? What recommendation would you make to him?

108

ON THE SCENE
Lesson opening scenario that provides motivation.

5.1 **FINANCE A BUSINESS**

in the business. Because the owner rather than the business is responsible for repaying the loan, that money is considered equity capital.

When one person owns a business, the sources of equity capital are limited to the resources of that individual. Often partnerships are formed so that two or more people can share the ownership and more financial resources are available to be invested in the business.

If a business makes a profit, those profits can be removed from the business for the personal use of the owners. If the profits remain in the business and are available to pay for business operations, they are known as *retained earnings*. Retained earnings are another source of equity capital.

Corporations sell stock to raise money for business operations. Stockholders are actually owners of a business. That means there are literally hundreds and thousands of owners of large corporations. The money people invest when they purchase stock is an important source of equity capital.

OBTAIN DEBT CAPITAL

When owners do not have additional money to invest in a business and retained earnings are not adequate, the business will need to borrow money if financing is needed. When a business needs a large amount of money to purchase a building or expensive equipment, it will need long-term financing. *Long-term financing* is a loan for more than a year and often for 10 to 20 years. For smaller amounts, or to obtain money to meet immediate needs, short-term financing is used. *Short-term financing* is a loan for less than a year and often must be repaid in 30 to 90 days.

The most common source of debt financing is a loan from a bank or other financial institution such as a mortgage company. A business that has a good financial record can obtain an *open line of credit*. That is a specific amount of money available to a business whenever financing is needed. The business has approval to write checks for any amount up to the limit established on the line of credit. An open line of credit is most often used for the expenses of normal business operations.

There are several other sources of debt capital. A vendor may grant credit as an incentive to purchase its products. The business may have 30 to 60 days to pay the bill, which is a form of a loan. If a business has a large amount of *accounts receivable*, or money owed to the business by its customers, it may sell those accounts to another company that will then collect the payments. The selling company will receive much less for the accounts than they are worth.

CHECKPOINT

What is the difference between equity capital and debt capital?

109

DID YOU KNOW?
Provides an interesting fact about the topic.

did you KNOW?

An Initial Public Offering (IPO) is the first time stock is made available for sale to the general public. New high-tech companies often use the IPO to raise money for operations.

CHECKPOINT
Short questions within lessons to assist with reading and to assure students are grasping concepts.

SPECIAL FEATURES ENHANCE LEARNING

COMMUNICATE
Provide activities to reinforce, review, and practice communication skills.

Some product liability lawsuits against companies for injuries suffered by consumers have resulted in settlements of hundreds of millions of dollars. Some companies have gone out of business as a result. Lawmakers in several states have proposed legislation to place a cap of a million dollars or less on the amount of money a company has to pay in such cases. Write a one-page paper in support of or opposing that legislation. Support your opinion with specific reasons.

BUSINESS MATH CONNECTION
Worked example that reinforces and reviews math concepts.

Calculate return on sales, inventory turnover, and return on investment for a business, assuming a net profit of $150,000, sales of $1,200,000, cost of goods sold of $400,000, average inventory of $120,000, and total assets of $600,000.

Return on sales = Net profit ÷ Sales

Inventory turnover = Cost of goods sold ÷ Average inventory

Return on investment = Net profit ÷ Total assets

SOLUTION

Return on sales = $150,000 ÷ $1,200,000 = 0.125 = 12.5%

Inventory turnover = $400,000 ÷ $120,000 = 3.33

Return on investment = $150,000 ÷ $600,000 = 0.25 = 25%

THINK CRITICALLY Do you think each of the ratios above indicate a strong financial performance? Why or why not?

WORKSHOP
Provides activities to use in class.

As a class, identify the sources of financing available to businesses in your community. You may want to use a telephone directory to help with the identification. Discuss the advantages and disadvantages of each source.

BANKS AND TECHNOLOGY Banks and other companies providing financial services are increasing their use of technology to deliver services. Consumers today can complete the following activities using their home computer.
- Pay bills
- Check account balances
- Obtain a credit card or loan
- Compare the cost of buying versus leasing an automobile
- Buy and sell stocks and mutual funds
- Transfer funds from one bank account to another
- File federal and state taxes

THINK CRITICALLY What additional financial services are available on the Internet?

TECH TALK
Provides information about new technology that is being used in business.

Dedicated web site b2000.swep.com that provides activities and links for each chapter.

GLOBAL TRADE EXPANSION

The Export-Import Bank of the United States encourages companies to sell products in other countries, especially developing nations. To increase exports the Bank offers a number of services to U.S. businesses. These include assisting businesses to obtain loans to produce exports, offering insurance to protect companies if international buyers do not pay for purchases, and extending credit to foreign buyers so they can purchase U.S. companies' products and services. An important reason the Export-Import Bank was developed was to create jobs in U.S. businesses.

THINK CRITICALLY How does financial support for exporting affect the number of people employed in the United States?

WORLD VIEW
Provides international business connections relevant to today's current events.

ASSESSMENT AND REVIEW

THINK CRITICALLY

1. What affect will the decision to not offer credit to customers have on a business?

_____

_____

_____

2. What steps can a person take to improve each of the four Cs of credit?

_____

_____

_____

_____

3. Why is it important for insurance companies to keep insurance premiums as low as possible?

_____

_____

_____

4. What are some examples of business risks that usually cannot be insured because they cannot be predicted?

_____

_____

_____

MAKE CONNECTIONS

5. TECHNOLOGY Use the Internet to locate a web site that compares the interest rates and annual fees charged to consumers for credit cards. List the three most inexpensive and the three most expensive credit cards.

_____

_____

_____

END-OF-LESSON ACTIVITIES

Think Critically Provides opportunities to apply concepts.

Make Connections Provides connections to other disciplines.

Presentation Icon indicates opportunity to use presentation software, such as PowerPoint.

Word Processing Icon indicates opportunity to use word processing software.

Spreadsheet Icon indicates opportunity to use spreadsheet software.

Internet Icon indicates opportunity to research on the web.

CHAPTER REVIEW
Contains Chapter Summary, Vocabulary Builder, Review Concepts, Apply What You Learned, Make Connections

---

REVIEW   CHAPTER 5

CHAPTER SUMMARY
LESSON 5.1 Finance a Business
A. The financial strength of a business is one of the most important factors to its success. Many businesses fail due to poor financial management.
B. When deciding on financing the important factors to consider are ownership, the cost of financing, and financing requirements.

LESSON 5.2 Financial Services
A. A business must manage its money wisely. Owners and managers are responsible for financial decisions. All businesses use the services of financial institutions.
B. Managers work with financial institutions to obtain and manage the money a business needs.

LESSON 5.3 Financial Records
A. Specific procedures, rules, and even laws must be followed in maintaining financial records so the records will be reliable.
B. Several important financial records are used by all businesses, including records of assets, receipts, payments, and payroll.

LESSON 5.4 Credit and Insurance
A. Businesses use credit when they make purchases and extend credit to customers to increase the volume of their sales.
B. Businesspeople must make careful plans to avoid risk or to be able to reduce the damage resulting from problems that occur.

VOCABULARY BUILDER
Choose the term that best fits the definition. Write the letter of the answer in the space provided. Some terms may not be used.

_____ 1. Organized summaries of a business's financial activities
_____ 2. Limits the amount of financial loss from an uncontrollable event in exchange for a regular payment of money
_____ 3. Money put in a financial institution that can be withdrawn at any time with no financial penalty
_____ 4. A specific, written financial plan
_____ 5. Money obtained from sources other than business owners
_____ 6. Money borrowed for a specific period of time on which interest must be paid
_____ 7. The financial resources used to operate a business
_____ 8. A person's ability to pay for credit extended
_____ 9. Financial resources provided by the owners of a business
_____ 10. Financial institutions regulated by state or federal governments that offer loan and deposit services

a. banks
b. budget
c. capital
d. credit-worthiness
e. debt capital
f. demand deposit
g. equity capital
h. financial records
i. insurance
j. loan

REVIEW CONCEPTS
11. What is the most common form of debt capital for a business?

_____

12. What are three important factors to consider when deciding on financing a business?

_____

APPLY WHAT YOU LEARNED
19. Why are stockholders considered owners of the business in which they have purchased stock?

_____

MAKE CONNECTIONS
23. ETHICS Many credit card companies send credit cards to people without checking their creditworthiness carefully. They hope the people will use the credit card, not pay off the balance, and then pay a high rate of interest on the balance. What is your view of that practice? How can consumers protect themselves against the practice? Should state or federal governments regulate that practice? Why or why not? Prepare to give a class presentation on this topic.

24. PERSONAL FINANCE Prepare a personal budget for one month using spreadsheet software. List the sources and anticipated amounts of income you will receive during the month. Then identify the major categories of expenses you will have and predict the amount you will spend in each category. After you have completed the budget, carefully track your income and expenses for one week and compare it to your budget. Write a brief statement describing how the budget compares to your actual financial performance.

25. BUSINESS COMMUNICATION You are the financial manager for the Action Company. One of your best customers, Jeb Yarcho, has fallen behind in making payments on the revolving credit account you have established for him. He has not made any payments for two months and has added an additional $500 of charges during that time. Using word processing software, write a letter requesting payment and offering to help if necessary. Make the letter positive, while communicating the serious nature of the problem.

26. TECHNOLOGY Use the Internet to find a web site that has a loan calculator. A loan calculator allows you to enter the amount of a loan, the length of the loan in months or years, and the interest rate. It will then calculate a monthly payment and the total amount of interest that must be paid during the time of the loan. Using the loan calculator, determine the monthly payment and total interest paid for different interest rates if $25,000 is borrowed for 5 years.

POINT YOUR BROWSER
b2000.swep.com

BUSINESS ENVIRONMENT AND OWNERSHIP 2

MANAGEMENT FUNCTIONS AND LEADERSHIP 28

COMMUNICATION AND INFORMATION SYSTEMS 56

PRODUCTION, MANUFACTURING, AND MARKETING 80

FINANCIAL MANAGEMENT 106

MANAGE HUMAN RESOURCES 132

REVIEWERS

Marilyn Allen
Hazelwood, MO

Sandra Bell-Duckworth
Westerville, OH

Rod Belnap
Ogden, UT

Angie Burlingame
Sugar Land, TX

Louis DiCesare
Rochester, NY

Eileen M. Dittmar
Grand Rapids, MI

Dee A. Fredrickson
Sugar Land, TX

Lisa Gil-de-Lamadrid
Miami, FL

Tomeka Hartsfield
Alexandria, VA

Frederick A. Nerone, Ph.D.
Naples, FL

Dennis L. Schmidt
Eustis, FL

Jennifer Wegner
Mishicot, WI

CHAPTER 1

BUSINESS ENVIRONMENT & OWNERSHIP

LESSONS

1.1 BUSINESS AND THE ECONOMY

1.2 FORMS OF OWNERSHIP

1.3 INTERNATIONAL BUSINESS

1.4 BUSINESS RESPONSIBILITY

PROJECT

Global Business in Your Life

PROJECT OBJECTIVES

■ Recognize the different types of businesses you can own and manage
■ Understand the differences between types of business ownership
■ Consider the factors that influence success in international business
■ Identify ethical responsibilities of businesses

GETTING STARTED

Read through the Project Process below. Make a list of any materials and information you will need. Decide how you will get the needed materials or information.
■ Identify three to five possible businesses you could own or manage related to your skills and interests.

PROJECT PROCESS

Part 1 **LESSON 1.1** In small groups, combine the lists of businesses you developed. Decide whether the businesses are producers and manufacturers, channel members, service businesses, or other types.

Part 2 **LESSON 1.2** Discuss the advantages and disadvantages of each type of ownership. Suggest which ownership form you would prefer for a business and the reasons for your decision.

Part 3 **LESSON 1.3** From your group's list of businesses, identify those the group agrees could be successful international businesses and those that might not be successful in other countries. Justify the decisions.

Part 4 **LESSON 1.4** Choose one business from your group list. Develop a Code of Ethics to guide business relationships with owners, employees, the community, customers, and other businesses.

CHAPTER REVIEW

Project Wrap-up Prepare group presentations. As a class, discuss the similarities and differences among the groups' businesses and decisions.

LESSON 1.1
BUSINESS AND THE ECONOMY

IDENTIFY the roles of business in the economy

DESCRIBE the responsibilities that accompany business ownership

BUSINESS AND THE ECONOMY

Businesses provide the products and services you need to live and enjoy your life. The types of businesses include producers and manufacturers, channel members, and service businesses. *Producers and manufacturers* convert raw materials into consumable products. *Channel members* add value to products as they move from the producer to consumers. That value is added by completing activities such as transportation, selling, promotion, and storage. *Service businesses* provide business activities that do not result in the ownership of anything tangible. Service businesses include theaters, insurance agencies, lawn care businesses, and many of the new businesses in the economy such as video stores, Internet web site designers, and financial advisors.

THE ROLE OF BUSINESS

Businesses are responsible for the standard of living you enjoy. They produce the products and services you consume every day. They also provide jobs for people. The wages people earn allow them to buy products and services.

ON THE $CENE

Jayson and Amee have heard that a large manufacturing business may relocate to their small town. They know that the jobs will be beneficial to the people living in the community. They also are aware that some manufacturers have been accused of polluting the air and rivers. They do not want their town and the lives of the people who live there to be negatively affected by the new business. What are the advantages and disadvantages a business brings to a community when it locates there?

If businesses do not produce the right products, consumers will be unable to satisfy some of their needs.

THE ROLE OF CONSUMERS

Consumers purchase and use the products and services produced by business. *Business consumers* are businesses that buy products and services for use in operating a business or to resell. *Final consumers* are individuals, families, or others who make purchases for their personal consumption. If consumers do not purchase the products offered by a company at a price that provides a profit, that company will not be able to continue to operate.

ECONOMIC PRINCIPLES

Several economic principles describe the relationship between businesses and consumers. The principle of **supply and demand** describes the relationship between production and consumption. Businesses make decisions about what they will produce or supply. Consumers make decisions on what to purchase or demand. If there is a greater supply of a product than demand, the price of the product will go down. If there is a greater demand by consumers than available supply, the price will go up.

The economic principle of *competition* means that many businesses can offer very similar products and services for sale. In order to encourage customers to purchase its product, a business must offer a greater value. Competition gives customers choices and encourages businesses to produce better and less expensive products.

Sometimes the economy becomes unbalanced. One or several businesses may take advantage of consumers. Businesses may be unable to offer a needed product profitably. Specific business operations may cause harm to people or the environment. In those situations, government regulation is necessary. *Government regulation* means that federal, state, or local governments pass laws or take steps to prevent harm to consumers, businesses, or the environment.

BUSINESS MATH CONNECTION

The table shows supply and demand for three given price levels. At which price level is supply and demand equal? What is the total amount consumers will spend and businesses will earn, at this level?

Price	Supply	Demand
$35	46,900	59,100
$38	51,350	51,350
$42	59,100	46,900

SOLUTION

Supply and demand are equal at the $38 price level. The formula for calculating how much consumers spend and businesses earn is

Supply or Demand × Price = Total amount
51,350 products × $38 = $1,951,300

CHECKPOINT ✓

What is the relationship between businesses and consumers in the economy?

BUSINESS RESPONSIBILITY

Businesses have the right to operate, to use resources, and to make a profit. Along with these rights is a set of responsibilities. Businesses have responsibilities to society, meaning the people in the city, state, or country in which they operate. They have a responsibility to the environment around them. They also have a responsibility to the owners and employees of the business. Finally, businesses are responsible to their customers and the other businesses with which they work.

SOCIAL RESPONSIBILITY

Social responsibility refers to the duty of a business to contribute to the well-being of society. Many businesses today are actively involved in their communities. They offer assistance to schools, community organizations, and local events and activities. They may provide that assistance by contributing money or by offering the time and knowledge of managers and employees. Businesses recognize that strong communities provide a better environment for business success. They also know that businesses can help develop and maintain strong communities. Examples of social responsibilities are contributing to charities, helping with community clean-ups and neighborhood restorations, and serving on citizen groups, such as school advisory committees.

ENVIRONMENTAL RESPONSIBILITY

Environmental responsibility refers to the duty of a business to protect the natural resources affected by its products and operations. The important natural resources of concern to all businesses are land, water, and air. Most businesses use other natural resources in operations as well, including minerals, trees, coal, oil, and natural gas.

A great deal of attention has been directed toward environmental pollution. Water pollution, the contamination of land by improper handling and disposal of chemicals and waste products, and problems with air quality are areas of concern. Businesses need to try to reduce pollution and protect the natural resources they use and the environment in which their employees and customers live.

RESPONSIBILITY TO OWNERS AND EMPLOYEES

Owners of a business invest money with the goal of making a profit. The managers of the business have a responsibility to use that money wisely.

Careless and risky business decisions can lead to a lack of profits, loss of money, and even business failure.

Businesses also have responsibilities to their employees. The primary responsibilities are to provide a safe work environment and a reasonable wage or salary for the employees' work. Employees should not be subject to harassment or discrimination because of age, gender, or ethnicity. Most businesspeople agree that businesses should try to maintain employees' jobs as long as they are productive and the business is profitable.

RESPONSIBILITY TO CUSTOMERS AND OTHER BUSINESSES

The final area of business responsibility is to those who support the business but are not a direct part of it. Customers are important to the success of every business. They should be treated fairly and provided complete and understandable information about the products and services they purchase. They also should receive adequate assistance if problems occur in the use of the products and services they buy.

A business also relies on other businesses for its success. Most businesses use suppliers to provide the products and services used in their operations. Most also work with banks and other financial institutions, utilities, transportation companies, advertising agencies, and many other types of businesses.

Businesses have the responsibility to cooperate and work effectively with the businesses that support their operations. If a business is dishonest in its relationships with other businesses, it will soon find that those businesses will choose not to cooperate. However, the business has the responsibility to be honest and ethical in all decisions and activities that can affect its competitors.

CHECKPOINT

Name the four areas of business responsibility.

_____

_____

THINK CRITICALLY

1. Why is the number of service businesses increasing faster in the U.S. than the number of other types of businesses?

_____

_____

_____

2. What are factors that would cause the supply of a particular product to increase or decrease? What would cause the demand for products to increase or decrease?

_____

_____

_____

3. Do you agree or disagree that the primary reason businesses exist is to make a profit? Explain your answer.

_____

_____

_____

4. Should state and federal governments pass laws to require businesses to be socially responsible? Why or why not?

_____

_____

_____

MAKE CONNECTIONS

5. **BUSINESS MATH** Using the following information, determine the price level at which supply and demand are equal. Then find the total amount that consumers will spend and businesses will earn at this level.

Price	Supply	Demand
$105	5,200	7,500
$120	6,400	6,400
$135	7,500	5,200

_____

_____

6. **SCIENCE** In small groups, brainstorm a list of ways that businesses can reduce pollution and protect the natural environment. Divide the list into those things a business can do that should not cost a great deal of money and those things that might be quite expensive for the business. Present your findings in a spreadsheet format.

7. **U.S. GOVERNMENT** Using the Internet or library resources, look up specific laws that regulate competition. Choose one of the laws, and write a one-page report about it. In your report include the name of the law, when it was enacted, and what businesses must do in order to comply with it.

LESSON 1.2
FORMS OF OWNERSHIP

COMPARE the three common forms of business ownership

DESCRIBE the steps to follow in starting a new business

ORGANIZE A BUSINESS

An **entrepreneur** is a person who takes the risk of starting and operating a business with the goal of making a profit. The risk occurs because entrepreneurs usually invest a large amount of their own money in the new business. They may lose the money if the business fails. A *manager* is a person who assumes responsibility for the successful operation of a business. Most managers are not entrepreneurs. They do not take the risk of investing their own money in the business. Other types of business owners invest some of their own money but do not actively participate in its operations.

The three common forms of business organization are proprietorships, partnerships, and corporations. The organization form determines who owns the business, the type of ownership risk, and the role of the owner in business operations.

ON THE $CENE

Jaimie Ortega has owned and operated a successful bakery for five years. He thinks he can increase the sales of his bakery products by developing an Internet site with online sales and overnight delivery. However, he knows the change in the business will require more money as well as expertise in e-commerce. Jaimie is faced with a difficult decision. Should he find a partner who can help develop the Internet business, find another way to get the necessary money and expertise, or forget the idea? What advice would you give him?

PROPRIETORSHIPS

The simplest and most common form of business ownership is the **proprietorship**. In a proprietorship, one person owns a business and takes the major responsibility for decisions about its operation. The owner of the business provides the resources and expertise needed to operate the business. In return, that person receives all of the profits earned by the business.

The primary advantage of a proprietorship is that it is very easy to form and operate. There are few legal requirements to start a business as a proprietorship. With enough money and expertise to start a business, anyone can become a business owner. As the sole owner, the person can make decisions quickly and be responsible for all areas of business operations.

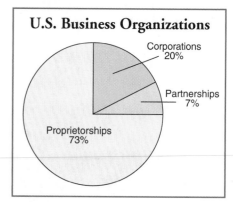

U.S. Business Organizations

Corporations 20%

Partnerships 7%

Proprietorships 73%

The primary disadvantage of this form of business organization is that the owner may not have the funds and expertise necessary to operate the business. There also is a high level of risk. If the business loses money, the owner is responsible for all losses. Finally, if something happens to the owner such as illness or death, it will be difficult for the business to continue.

PARTNERSHIPS

To overcome some of the disadvantages of proprietorships, some businesses are organized as partnerships. In a **partnership**, the business is owned by two or more people who share the risks, rewards, and responsibility for operations. There are fewer partnerships than other forms of business organizations. The partnership often is chosen by people who provide professional services such as physicians, lawyers, and accountants. It also is chosen by owners of proprietorships who look for partners when they want to expand.

The advantages of a partnership are that more resources and expertise are available and that risk is shared. The business also is more likely to continue if something happens to one owner. Disadvantages result when the owners disagree on how to operate the business. Profits must be shared by all partners and each partner is responsible for all debts of the business. If one partner is unable to pay his or her share of debts, all other partners must make up that portion. Finally, if one partner leaves the business, it may be difficult to find another partner.

CORPORATIONS

Most large businesses and some small businesses are organized as corporations. In a **corporation**, a number of people own the business through the purchase of stock but have limited responsibility and liability. Some people refer to a corporation as an "artificial person." State laws allow a corporation to borrow money, sign contracts, and own property. A corporation can make a profit, lose money, and pay taxes. Corporations cannot operate without a *charter*. This is a legal document issued by a state granting the business the power to organize, issue stock, and complete specific activities.

Corporations have several advantages. A corporation has access to more money through the sale of stock. The business may have many owners because a person can invest in the business by purchasing only a few shares of stock. The risk of ownership is much less in a corporation. Laws limit the liability of most stockholders to the amount of their investment. Many corporations hire managers who are responsible for day-to-day operations so the owners do not have to be business experts. Corporations also are the most stable form of business organization because ownership is easily transferred from one person to another. Disadvantages of corporations include a lack of responsibility for business success as a result of many owners, higher taxes paid by corporations, and greater government regulation of operations.

What are the three forms of business organization?

_____

_____

START A NEW BUSINESS

In the United States and other countries with free market economies, it is easy to start a new business. There are tens of thousands of small businesses. They are started by men, women, teenagers, and older people in their retirement years. Entrepreneurship is a dream shared by many. Understanding and carefully following the correct steps can lead to successful business ownership.

It is easy to start a business but difficult to make the business successful. Most new businesses fail because of poor planning. Time should be spent gathering information and making the right decisions about business organization and operations.

DETERMINE A NEED

A business must have customers who want to buy the products and services offered and have the money to buy them. A new business should not be faced with such strong competition from other businesses that it will be difficult to make a profit. The first step in starting a business is to study customers and competitors to make sure there is a good business opportunity.

DEVELOP A BUSINESS PLAN

A **business plan** is a written description of the business and its operations with an analysis of its strengths and the risks it faces. Preparing a written plan helps to insure that the owner has carefully considered the important decisions necessary to start and operate the business. It also is a good reference for the owner and others as the business grows. The business plan should be reviewed and updated regularly.

In a recent year, 155,141 new businesses were started. In the same year, 71,857 businesses failed. The number of business failures was 46 percent of the number of startups.

> ## BUSINESS PLAN OUTLINE
> ## FOR A NEW BUSINESS
>
> **Overview of the Business**
> - ■ Business description, goals, and objectives
> - ■ Characteristics of the economy
> - ■ Identification and analysis of customers and competition
>
> **Business Operations**
> - ■ Organization of the business
> - ■ Description of operations
> - ■ Personnel, equipment, and resources needed
>
> **Marketing Activities**
> - ■ Market characteristics and needs
> - ■ Product, distribution, pricing, and promotion decisions
>
> **Financial Plan**
> - ■ Startup costs
> - ■ Income, expense, and cash flow projections
> - ■ Budgets for 1 to 3 years
>
> **Sources of Financing**

OBTAIN FINANCING

With a business plan, the business owner will know how much money is needed to start and operate the business. For a very small business, the owner may have enough money saved to finance the business. However, most businesses need additional financing to be able to operate until the business is profitable. The common types of financing for new businesses are borrowing from friends and family members, obtaining bank loans, taking one or more partners into the business, or selling stock.

There are advantages and disadvantages to each type of financing. It is not easy to obtain the money needed to start a business. Anyone asked to invest in a business will want to make sure the business will be successful so they will not lose their money.

MEET LEGAL REQUIREMENTS

Federal, state, and local governments have laws businesses must follow in starting and operating a business. It is the responsibility of the business owner to be familiar with and follow the laws. Most new owners work with a lawyer to make sure all legal requirements are met.

Forms of Business Organization Each form of business ownership has different legal requirements. There are few requirements to start a business as a proprietorship because only one person is involved as an owner. A partnership requires a *partnership agreement*, a contract describing the relationship and responsibilities of each partner. Corporations are bound by the charter issued by the state in which the business is started and by the laws specifically written to regulate corporations. Corporations have annual reports and records that must be prepared and filed.

COMMUNICATE

Think of a new business you would like to start and the reasons it should be successful. Then identify several things you would need to open and operate the business that would require a bank loan. For example, you might need to purchase or rent a building and equipment.

Prepare a short oral presentation to convince a banker to make a loan to you. Remember the banker will need to understand the business, your need for the loan, and why the loan will not be a risky investment. Give your presentation in class.

Business Regulations

Laws affect many business activities. Businesses need special licenses to operate. Most businesses must collect and pay taxes. Zoning laws identify where specific types of business can operate. Environmental regulations affect the use of water, the type of energy a business can use, and the need for special equipment to reduce pollution.

OPEN THE BUSINESS

The work of business owners is just beginning when the business plan is completed and financing is obtained. Decisions must be made on how the work will be accomplished, who will do the work, and how to be sure that customers are satisfied and the business is profitable. Finally equipment, materials, and supplies must be obtained so the business can operate.

Organize the Business A new business may start out with the owner doing all of the work. However, it won't be long before there is more work than one person can handle or activities that the owner does not know how to do. As a business grows, work must be organized to make sure it is done well.

Organizing is done by dividing the operations of the business into departments or among employees and assigning responsibilities for each type of work. Most large businesses have an *organization chart*, a visual device that shows the structure of the organization, the division of work, and the relationships among employees.

Prepare Employees People are one of the most important resources a business has. Employees are responsible for getting work done well. A business owner needs to identify what types of employees to hire, the qualifications required, and how much to pay them. Once employees are hired, they will usually need training to perform their duties well. The business owner will need to be an effective manager and leader to motivate employees and to develop a good working environment.

Meet Customer Needs The final step in starting a new business is operating the business in a way that satisfies customers. A satisfied customer will return to the business in the future and will tell others about the business. Customers do not always buy products with the lowest prices. They want a quality product and effective service at a good price.

WORKSHOP

There is a high failure rate among new businesses. In small groups, review the steps in starting a new business described in the lesson. Discuss the importance of each step. Then, working alone, rank the steps from most important to least important to the success of a business. Discuss your rankings in your groups and justify your decisions.

CHECKPOINT

To open a business, in what three areas must decisions be made?

_____

_____

THINK CRITICALLY

1. Why are there more proprietorships in the U.S. than partnerships and corporations?

_____

_____

_____

2. Why might a person who owns a growing proprietorship choose to hire a manager to help operate the business rather than find a partner to invest in the business?

_____

_____

_____

3. Why do you think there are more legal requirements for a corporation than for a partnership or proprietorship?

_____

_____

_____

MAKE CONNECTIONS

4. **TECHNOLOGY** The Internet has become an important place for new businesses to operate. It is possible for a very small business to compete against larger businesses and serve customers worldwide. Use the Internet to locate 10 different businesses. Identify the products or services they sell. For each, develop a short statement describing why you think it will or will not be a successful business. Then write another statement justifying whether or not you think the business would be of interest to customers from other countries.

_____

_____

_____

_____

5. **FINANCE** Use the Internet or a newspaper to find the stock prices of several corporations. Identify a high-priced stock, a moderately priced stock, and a low-priced stock. Use a spreadsheet to organize the information you find. Assuming you had $1,000 to invest, which of the three stocks would you choose to own? Why?

_____

_____

_____

_____

LESSON 1.3
INTERNATIONAL BUSINESS

DESCRIBE important characteristics of international trade

IDENTIFY procedures businesses can follow to identify international business opportunities

INTERNATIONAL TRADE

If you are traveling in another state and stop to make a purchase, you probably won't give much thought to the experience. The products will be familiar to you. You can use the same money you use in your own state. And the businessperson probably speaks the same language as you do. If you travel to a different country, your experience might be quite different. The country will have different laws and regulations for business. You will see products different from those you typically use. The people might speak another language and use a different currency. This example shows the potential difficulty of international business. *International business* refers to any business activities that occur between two or more countries. Due to advances in transportation, communications, and business practices, international businesses has become very important.

ON THE $CENE

Jacob Greenspan woke up and prepared for a day at school. He was not aware of the many ways international business affected his life. His toothpaste was produced by a company headquartered in England. His clothes were manufactured in Vietnam and China. For breakfast, the wheat used to produce his cereal was grown in Canada and the fruit came from Costa Rica. Jacob's father drove him to school in their Japanese car. During his first class, the teacher showed a video using a Korean TV while Jacob took notes on his laptop computer assembled in Mexico. Jacob's life would be very different without international business. What affect does international business have on you?

IMPORTS AND EXPORTS

International trade occurs when people from one country buy from or sell to people in another country. Products that are purchased from another country are known as **imports**. Products sold to customers in another country are known as **exports**. Both imports and exports are important to a country. Some countries have many more imports than exports. They are sending a large amount of money to other countries rather than using it to support their own businesses. Other countries have many more exports than imports. In those countries consumers will have fewer choices and may pay higher prices for the goods and services they buy.

The difference between a country's imports and exports is known as the *balance of trade*. In a recent year the United States had $956 billion in exports and $1.2 trillion in imports. That meant the U.S. had a negative balance of trade—more imports than exports.

U.S. TRADE WITH OTHER COUNTRIES (1998, in millions)

Country	Exports	Imports
Australia	$ 14,216	$ 5,387
Brazil	15,142	10,102
Canada	$156,603	173,256
England	39,058	34,838
Japan	57,831	121,845
Mexico	78,773	94,629
Russia	3,553	5,747

MOVE INTO INTERNATIONAL BUSINESS

Many companies do not consider participating in international trade until they discover a need. If a company is having difficulty selling its products or wants to increase sales, it may attempt to sell its products in another country. In the same way, a business that cannot find a specific product it needs in its own country may turn to foreign countries to locate the product. Once companies begin to trade with businesses from other countries, they usually continue and expand the amount of international business they do.

TRAINING FOR GLOBAL CAREERS

Many people who work for international businesses are asked to work in another country. The assignment may last for several years and will often be in a country with a different culture and language. Companies offer training for the employee and family members who will be relocating. Part of the training is learning to speak and write the new language. The training also emphasizes day-to-day situations employees and their families will encounter. Everyone is prepared to understand and participate in the new community. A recent addition to international business training is called *reorientation*. This takes place at the end of the assignment. The company helps employees and their families to learn about changes that have occurred while they were away and to adjust to the return.

THINK CRITICALLY Assume you are responsible for preparing people to live in your community after having been away for several years. What would you include in the training?

It is usually easier to sell products in other countries if there is a cooperating business in that country. Specialized businesses provide exporting and importing services including buying and selling, banking, and transportation.

CHECKPOINT

Name three ways a business can participate in international business.

_____

_____

_____

INTERNATIONAL BUSINESS OPPORTUNITIES

International business presents both opportunities and challenges to businesspeople. Fair competition among businesses from many countries encourages companies to make product improvements, reduce prices, and meet customer needs. You would not have many of the products and services you enjoy each day without international trade.

Companies should not avoid opportunities in international business just because they have not had previous experience outside their own country. On the other hand, a move into international business should be approached carefully to make sure it is successful.

Before conducting business in another country, business owners and managers should carefully study to make sure a market exists for the company's products and services. Taking the following steps will help a business decide whether or not to participate in international business.

1. Select countries or regions to study

2. Complete market research

3. Identify social, cultural, and economic differences and similarities

4. Review laws and regulations

5. Identify resources that provide assistance

6. Develop an international business plan

WORKSHOP

A company from another country has asked your class to help it identify opportunities to sell products to high school students in your state. What advice would you give them about unique social, cultural, and economic factors that affect what students buy and how they buy?

CHECKPOINT

What is the last step a company should take to move into international business?

_____

_____

THINK CRITICALLY

1. Why do you think that many companies choose not to engage in international business?

2. What do you think are the advantages and disadvantages of conducting international business by working with a cooperating business in another country?

3. What factors do you think should be considered in selecting countries or regions for study when identifying international business opportunities?

MAKE CONNECTIONS

4. BUSINESS MATH Use the information from the chart on page 16 entitled U.S. Trade With Other Countries. Using spreadsheet software, determine the balance of trade for each country listed and if the balance is positive or negative. Calculate the total amount of U.S. exports and imports for the countries listed and the total balance of trade. Determine whether the total balance is positive or negative.

5. SOCIAL STUDIES Many products first developed in the United States have become very popular in other countries while others are not well accepted. In small groups, develop a list of the types of products that seem to be accepted in other cultures and those that are not well accepted. Use newspapers, magazines, and the Internet to gather information to help you develop the lists. Review the two lists and determine factors that might affect the acceptance of products in other countries. Give group presentations of your findings to the class.

LESSON 1.4
BUSINESS RESPONSIBILITY

GOALS

IDENTIFY important areas of the law that affect businesses

DESCRIBE how businesspeople can encourage ethical decisions and actions

BUSINESS LAW

A *democracy* is a form of government that offers a great deal of freedom yet provides protection when individuals or groups can suffer from the actions of others. Laws and regulations have been developed to maintain the balance between the freedoms of individuals and organizations and the harm that can be faced because of the actions of others.

In the U.S. economy, businesses and consumers are free to make decisions about what is produced and what is consumed. Government regulation is used to prevent harm to consumers, businesses, and the environment. The areas of government regulation dealing with business-to-business and business-to-consumer relationships is known as *business law.*

ON THE $CENE

Recently Microsoft Corporation was taken to court by the federal government. The company was accused of unfair business practices that prevented other businesses from competing successfully, resulting in fewer choices and higher prices for consumers. The lawsuit asked the courts to break the large company into two or more smaller independent businesses that would compete against each other and with other software development companies. Microsoft attorneys argued that their company was an example of the American dream. The entrepreneur Bill Gates started a small company whose products were very successful. It grew to become a large and profitable business. Attorneys suggested many companies had the same opportunity and Microsoft's success had actually resulted in better products and lower prices for consumers. Do you agree with the government lawyers or Microsoft's? Explain your answer.

REGULATE COMPETITION

Competition is a cornerstone of a free market economy. Because of competition, businesses must find ways to offer better products, better service, and better prices to consumers. As a result of competition, consumers have more information and more choices when they purchase products and services. Laws have been developed to encourage competition and to carefully regulate business practices in situations where there is little competition.

Monopolies A *monopoly* exists when only one company provides a product or service without competition from other companies. In a monopoly, a business does not have to offer customers a good value or improve its products and services. Consumers are at the mercy of the business. If consumers need the product, they can purchase it at only one place.

Laws have been passed to prevent most monopolies. If a company dominates a market and prevents other businesses from competing, the government will step in to change the conditions in the market. The business may have to sell parts of its operations or change its practices that reduce competition. The government watches carefully when a large company wants to purchase a competing company. The purchase may be prevented if it appears the new larger company will have too much control of the market.

From time to time, circumstances are identified where a monopoly is judged to be appropriate. For example it is very expensive to provide water, electricity, and natural gas to all households in a city. The cost of water treatment facilities, water and gas lines, and energy-generating plants is very high. One company may be granted a monopoly by the government to build the infrastructure and provide the needed service. However the level of service and prices will be closely monitored and regulated by the government.

Unfair Business Practices One business may try to take advantage of other businesses by using unfair business practices. Government agencies have been created with the responsibility for overseeing businesses and preventing those unfair practices.

The Federal Trade Commission (FTC) is the primary agency monitoring business practices. They look for illegal practices that give one business too much control over other businesses. Those practices include unfair pricing, agreements among several businesses to take advantage of consumers or other businesses, false or misleading advertising, and misuse of patents and copyrights.

There are many other federal agencies with responsibility for areas of business law and regulation. They include the Federal Communications Commission (FCC), the Food and Drug Administration (FDA), the Securities and Exchange Commission (SEC), the Equal Employment Opportunity Commission (EEOC), and the Internal Revenue Service (IRS). State and local governments also regulate business practices and an increasing number of international organizations have responsibilities for the growing amount of trade between countries.

PROVIDE CONSUMER PROTECTION

Government is concerned that consumers have choices of products and services and can make informed decisions about what to buy. The greatest area of concern for consumer protection is *product safety*. People want to be assured that food they consume and products they purchase are safe. Businesses must clearly demonstrate that materials and ingredients they use meet established standards and that products will not harm the consumer.

A second area is *product availability and price.* Businesses cannot unfairly prevent people from obtaining the product or charge one group of consumers more for the same product. For example the manager of an apartment building cannot discriminate in renting the apartment.

Finally, consumers should have *access to adequate and accurate information* in order to make good decisions about the products and services they buy. Government agencies regulate product labeling, how prices are calculated and communicated to consumers, the amount and type of product information that must be provided, and accuracy in advertising.

CHECKPOINT

What types of protection are offered to businesses and consumers through business law?

_____

_____

BUSINESS ETHICS

Laws are developed to hold businesses and individuals responsible for activities and behavior that have been judged to be harmful or dangerous. On a day-to-day basis, businesspeople are called on to make decisions or take actions that may be legal but which many people would consider to be inappropriate. Ethics as well as laws should guide decisions and actions.

Ethics are the principles, beliefs, and values accepted by a society or culture that guide the conduct of individuals and groups. The beliefs and values often are unwritten but well understood. Individuals are exposed to important values as children by parents and other adults. They learn "right from wrong" in their homes, schools, and other institutions.

Business ethics are principles of conduct guiding the actions of businesspeople. Often business associations develop written statements of ethical beliefs and practices known as a *code of ethics.* The associations then use the code of ethics to identify businesses and individuals who are ethical or unethical in their practices.

ETHICAL DILEMMAS FACING BUSINESSES

Acting ethically is not easy. Often there is a conflict between what is right, what others expect you to do, and what seems best for the business. Also, people do not always agree on the most ethical decisions and actions. Differences among countries and cultures, religions, and even different generations affect perceptions of ethical behavior. Consider the following ethical situations and how they might affect the actions of a businessperson.

In small groups, choose one of the ethical dilemmas businesses face. Make up a role-play scenario to illustrate the ethical dilemma. Perform your role-plays in class.

ETHICS AND THE INTERNET The Internet presents a whole new set of ethical issues for businesses. The Computer Professionals for Social Responsibility (CPSR) has developed a Code of Fair Information Practices to help businesspeople make good decisions on the use of the Internet. The Code includes the following points

■ Personal information obtained for one purpose should not be used for another purpose without informed consent.

■ Collect only the information necessary for a particular purpose. Dispose of personally identifying information whenever possible.

■ Ensure the accuracy, reliability, and timeliness of personal information.

■ Establish and enforce an information privacy policy and make the policy publicly available.

THINK CRITICALLY Do you think the Code of Fair Information Practices will be effective in protecting the privacy of consumers? Why or why not?

Use of Natural Resources A business must use natural resources such as trees, water, or petroleum as a part of its operations. However, unwise use of the resources can result in pollution, damage to the environment, or a decreasing supply of those resources.

Fair Treatment of Employees and Customers Many business decisions affect employees and customers. A business may decide to close a plant in the U.S. and move the jobs to another country. Some businesses do not give women and ethnic minorities equal opportunities for job advancement. Businesspeople may decide to halt production and distribution of a product that may harm customers even though it means the company will lose money.

Relationships with Other Businesses Many business relationships are protected by laws but some activities must be judged as ethical or unethical even if they are legal. A large business can easily force a smaller company out of business by cutting its prices until the small business fails. Businesses decide whether to work cooperatively and openly with their suppliers and other supporting businesses or to be less than honest in those relationships.

Differences among Countries and Cultures In some countries, businesses expect to give large gifts or even bribes to officials to obtain favorable treatment. In developing economies, people may be willing to work for very low wages. This allows employers to earn greater profits than they would if they paid employees a reasonable wage.

What are three ethical dilemmas a business might face?

_____

_____

THINK CRITICALLY

1. Why is there a need for government regulation of business activities?

_____

_____

_____

2. Why are fewer regulated monopolies, such as telephone and electric service, granted by local governments today than in the past?

_____

_____

_____

3. How can a business activity be unethical even if it is legal?

_____

_____

_____

_____

MAKE CONNECTIONS

4. BUSINESS LAW Review newspaper and magazine articles to find three examples of business laws. For each one identified, determine the type of business activities affected by the law.

_____

_____

_____

_____

5. U.S. GOVERNMENT Use the Internet to locate each of the following federal agencies and determine how each agency regulates business practices: (a) Federal Trade Commission, (b) Federal Communication Commission, (c) Equal Employment Opportunity Commission, (d) Food and Drug Administration. Write a paragraph explaining your findings for each agency.

_____

_____

_____

_____

_____

6. COMMUNICATION In small groups, create a code of ethics for students in your school. Develop at least five statements of beliefs and values for the code of ethics. Prepare your group's code of ethics document on a computer using word processing software. Compare your code with those of other groups. Discuss how a code of ethics could be used to influence student behavior in your school.

REVIEW

CHAPTER SUMMARY

LESSON 1.1 Business and the Economy

A. Businesses are responsible for the standard of living you enjoy by producing the products, services, and employment opportunities.

B. While businesses have a right to make a profit, they also have responsibilities to the community and people who live there.

LESSON 1.2 Forms of Ownership

A. The three common types of business ownership are proprietorships, partnerships, and corporations.

B. Planning a new business includes gathering information and making the right decisions about business organization and operations.

LESSON 1.3 International Business

A. Once companies begin to trade with businesses from other countries, they usually continue and expand the amount of international business they do.

B. Before conducting business in another country, a business should make sure a market exists for its products and services in that country.

LESSON 1.4 Business Responsibility

A. Ethics are principles of morality and rules of conduct. Codes of ethics are written to guide the activity of individuals within a company.

B. Social responsibility is the obligation of a business to contribute to the well-being of a community.

VOCABULARY BUILDER

Choose the term that best fits the definition. Write the letter of the answer in the space provided. Some terms may not be used.

_____ **1.** Those who purchase or use products and services

_____ **2.** The relationship between production and consumption

_____ **3.** A person who takes the risk of starting and operating a business with the goal of making a profit

_____ **4.** One person owns a business and takes the major responsibility for decisions about its operation

_____ **5.** Business owned by two or more people who share the risks, rewards, and responsibility

_____ **6.** Business owned by a number of people who purchase shares of stock but who have limited responsibility and liability

_____ **7.** Products purchased from another country

_____ **8.** Products sold to customers in another country

_____ **9.** The principles, beliefs, and values accepted by a society or culture that guide the conduct of individuals and groups

_____ **10.** A written description of the business and its operations with an analysis of its strengths and the risks it faces

a. business plan
b. consumers
c. corporation
d. entrepreneur
e. ethics
f. exports
g. imports
h. partnership
i. proprietorship
j. supply and demand

POINT YOUR BROWSER

b2000.swep.com

REVIEW CONCEPTS

11. What is the role of consumers in the economy?

_____

_____

_____

12. What are the important areas of responsibility for businesses?

_____

_____

_____

13. What are three common forms of business organization?

_____

_____

_____

14. What is the important first step in developing a new business?

_____

_____

_____

15. How is a country's balance of trade determined?

_____

_____

_____

16. Why is it important to identify the social, cultural, and economic differences of a country before deciding to engage in international trade?

_____

_____

_____

17. What are the benefits of competition in a capitalistic economy?

_____

_____

_____

18. What are the ethical dilemmas faced by many businesses?

_____

_____

_____

APPLY WHAT YOU LEARNED

19. What are some examples of products and services for which you often see the price change as a result of supply and demand?

_____

_____

_____

_____

20. Why do you think there are more proprietorships than corporations when corporations are much larger and more profitable than most proprietorships?

_____

_____

_____

_____

21. In what ways can the Internet be helpful to a company that wants to become involved in international business?

_____

_____

_____

_____

22. Should the government break up very large companies that have been able to gain control of a large share of a market? Why or why not?

_____

_____

_____

_____

MAKE CONNECTIONS

23. BUSINESS MATH If there are 23,250,000 businesses in the United States, how many businesses are organized as proprietorships, partnerships, and corporations based on the following percentages? Use spreadsheet software, if available, to compute your answers.

Type of Organization	Percent of Businesses	Number of Businesses
Proprietorships	73%	_____
Partnerships	7%	_____
Corporations	20%	_____

24. PROBLEM SOLVING The balance of trade is very important to U.S. government officials. If the United States has a negative balance of trade, it is sending more money to other countries to purchase products and services than it is receiving from the sale of its products and services. That means the businesses from other countries have more money to invest in businesses and jobs and U.S. businesses will have less to invest. Some officials think laws should be passed to limit trade with countries who do not buy from the United States. Others think the U.S. should help its businesses by providing marketing assistance and even financial incentives to increase international trade. How do you think the balance of trade problem should be handled? How do you think the U.S. can improve its balance of trade? Using a computer and word processing program, write a one-page report on your ideas. Make the outline for your report on the lines that follow.

_____

_____

_____

_____

_____

25. ETHICS You are the human resources manager of a large business. In a meeting of the company's managers, you have been told that the business is going to have to close one of its locations due to high labor costs. The jobs will be moved to a new operation in another country. However you have been told you cannot tell employees of the planned closing because it might cause them to be very dissatisfied, not be as concerned about the quality of their work, and quit their jobs long before the location will close. Identify the ethical dilemma you face as a manager and describe what you would do. Justify your solution. Present your answers in a report to the class.

26. CAREERS Most businesspeople think there is a great difference in the personal characteristics of an entrepreneur and a manager. Work with a small group and develop a list of the characteristics important for a successful entrepreneur and those important for a business manager. Compare the lists and note similarities and differences. Locate information on the Internet and use library resources such as business books and magazines that describe the characteristics of entrepreneurs and managers. Compare that information with the lists your group developed.

_____

_____

_____

_____

_____

CHAPTER 2

MANAGEMENT FUNCTIONS & LEADERSHIP

LESSONS

CAREERS IN BUSINESS

SAS INSTITUTE, INC.

SAS Institute is a rapidly growing computer software development business. From its campus located in Cary, NC, it helps businesses gather and analyze information to improve decisions. Recently SAS began developing Internet-delivered instructional materials for schools. SAS has been recognized for many years as one of the top companies to work for in the U.S. It recently was listed as one of the top 100 businesses providing excellent customer service.

Consulting Project Managers at SAS manage complex consulting projects with clients. They coordinate the work of SAS Group Managers and all departments involved. They also interact with many people in the client's organization. The managers need a bachelor's degree in business or computer science, five years of customer support or sales experience, and experience managing team projects. Problem-solving and communications skills are important in this job.

THINK CRITICALLY

1. Why would a manager choose a career at SAS Institute rather than another company?
2. How can customer support and sales experience contribute to the development of management skills?

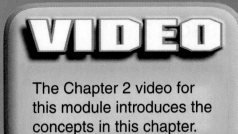
VIDEO

The Chapter 2 video for this module introduces the concepts in this chapter.

PROJECT
Understand Management

PROJECT OBJECTIVES

■ Understand how managers affect the success of a business
■ Recognize the characteristics of effective leaders
■ Determine how managers plan, organize, implement, and control

GETTING STARTED

Read through the Project Process below. Make a list of materials and information you will need. Decide how you will get the needed materials or information.
■ Select a business you would like to start that requires several managers to be effective.
■ Find one or more working adults willing to be interviewed.

PROJECT PROCESS

Part 1 LESSON 2.1 For the business you selected, make a list of the activities managers will need to do to make the business successful.

Part 2 LESSON 2.2 Ask several working adults to identify what they think are the characteristics of a good leader. Review all of the responses and select the leadership characteristics identified by more than one person.

Part 3 LESSON 2.3 Use the list of activities completed in Part 1 to identify all of the planning and organizing activities the managers of your business must complete. Add activities to the list if necessary.

Part 4 LESSON 2.4 Use the list of activities completed in Part 1 to identify all of the implementing and controlling activities the managers of your business must complete. Add activities to the list if necessary.

CHAPTER REVIEW

Project Wrap-up Using the information you found, prepare job descriptions for at least three management positions for your company. The job description should list the job duties to be performed, education needed, and work experience required. Compare your job descriptions with those developed by other students.

LESSON 2.1
THE MANAGER'S ROLE

IDENTIFY what managers do and how their work is different from employees' work

DESCRIBE important management principles and the steps in problem solving

THE WORK OF MANAGERS

The work of managers is important to business success. Though non-management employees complete most of the day-to-day work, managers make things happen in business. They are responsible for the success or failure of the company. The decisions managers make determine what a company will do and how well it will perform.

Management is the process of accomplishing the goals of an organization through the effective use of people and other resources. Those resources include money, buildings, equipment, and materials. Operating a business is a complex process. If managers are not well prepared to operate the business, problems will soon develop. The person who understands the responsibilities of management and how to work effectively with people usually will be a successful manager.

ON THE $CENE

Arlene Errinson has been a successful accountant for CountTemp for the past eight years. She enjoys her work but is not as challenged as she once was. She has just been asked to apply for the position of Senior Accountant. This means she will be responsible for managing a staff of 10 accountants and their 6 assistants. Her work would change dramatically because she would supervise the work of others on a daily basis rather than completing accounting work. She would be responsible for the amount and the quality of other people's work rather than just her own. How should Arlene decide if the manager's job is what she really wants to do?

The primary work of all managers can be grouped within four functions. **Planning** involves analyzing information and making decisions about what needs to be done. **Organizing** is determining how plans can be accomplished most effectively and arranging resources to complete work. Managers are **implementing** when they carry out the plans and help employees to work effectively. They are **controlling** when they evaluate results to determine if the company's objectives have been accomplished as planned.

MANAGEMENT AND NON-MANAGEMENT WORK

You can probably think of work employees do that involves planning, organizing, implementing, and controlling. For example, most people are asked to carefully plan their work activities and organize the materials and resources they use. Members of a work team may be responsible for implementing a major new project and evaluating the success of the project when they are finished. In these examples, employees are taking responsibility for their work. They also are getting valuable experience that can be helpful if they become managers. However, even though employees perform some work that is similar to managers' responsibilities, the employees are not managers.

Managers complete all four management functions on a regular basis. They also have authority over other jobs and people. In each situation where employees complete what seem to be management functions, they spend less time on those activities than on their other job responsibilities. They also cannot assume authority over other employees. Finally, they are not completing all of the functions regularly.

A company collected information from its managers about the type of work they completed each week. The results showed the average manager spent the following hours on each of the management functions.

Planning = 8 hours   Implementing = 18 hours
Organizing = 12 hours   Controlling = 10 hours

On average, how many total hours each week do the managers work? What percentage of the workweek does the average manager devote to each of the management functions?

SOLUTION

To find the total hours, add the hours for each function.

Planning + Organizing + Implementing + Controlling = Total hours
8 hours + 12 hours + 18 hours + 10 hours = 48 hours

To find the percentage, divide the hours spent on each function by the total hours worked.

Planning   8 hours ÷ 48 hours = 16.7%
Organizing   12 hours ÷ 48 hours = 25%
Implementing   18 hours ÷ 48 hours = 37.5%
Controlling   10 hours ÷ 48 hours = 20.8%

LEVELS OF MANAGEMENT

Most companies typically have more than one level of management. Large companies may have five or six management levels. Today many companies are attempting to reduce the number of management levels, making each level of management and each manager's work more important. This allows employees to take more responsibility for their own work and to complete more of the duties that were the responsibility of managers in the past.

A manager whose main job is to direct the work of employees is called a *supervisor.* Supervisors are the first level of management in a company and usually spend some of their time completing non-management activities. A *middle manager* completes all of the management functions, but spends most of the time on one management function such as planning or controlling. A middle manager also may be responsible for a specific part of the company's operations such as sales or information management. An *executive* is a top-level manager who spends most of his or her time on management functions.

As managers move from working as a supervisor to higher levels of management, the functions on which they spend the most time change. Supervisors work directly with employees and make sure that the day-to-day work of the business is completed. Therefore, they devote most of their management time to implementing. Middle managers develop plans for their part of the company and decide how to implement those plans. Executives work with other managers and are responsible for the long-term direction of the business. They spend most of their time on planning and controlling activities.

CHECKPOINT

What are the four functions of management?

_____

_____

EFFECTIVE MANAGEMENT

Today's managers know that employees are motivated to do their best when they are treated fairly and think they are an important part of the business. Good managers respect their employees, involve them in decisions about how work will be done, and provide recognition and rewards when employees do a good job.

MANAGEMENT PRINCIPLES

There are three important principles of management that result in good working relationships between managers and employees. The first principle, *span of control,* is the number of employees who report to one manager. Managers should have a limited number of people for whom they are responsible to give each employee the necessary help and attention.

A second principle of management is *unity of command.* That principle means that each employee should have only one manager. If an employee has more than one manager, it is easy to become confused if there are conflicts in assignments and instructions.

Authority and responsibility is the third management principle. Managers assign employees responsibilities or work duties to perform. Managers also give employees the authority to complete those responsibilities. Authority means that the employee can make the decisions needed to complete the work without having to check with the manager.

MAKE DECISIONS AND SOLVE PROBLEMS

Managers are responsible for making decisions and solving problems. While good managers involve employees in problem solving, the manager is held accountable for the result of the decision.

Scientific Problem Solving Most decisions are made by completing a series of steps known as *scientific problem solving.* You may have had experience with this procedure in science classes. The procedure works as well for businesspeople as it does for scientists. The steps in scientific problem solving are listed below.

1. Identify the problem.

2. List possible solutions.

3. Carefully analyze the possible solutions.

4. Select the best solution using the results of the analysis.

A problem is a difficult situation requiring a solution. Businesses are faced with many problems. Managers need to be prepared to recognize important problems and follow a careful decision-making process to identify the best possible solution.

Business problems are not always easy to identify. Often a situation will appear to be the problem when it is only a symptom of a bigger problem. The business will not improve unless the real problem is recognized. Managers must carefully gather and study information to identify possible solutions. They need to be objective. Otherwise they might misinterpret the information and arrive at the wrong solution.

After selecting the best solution, the manager must determine how it will be implemented. The problem is not solved just because a solution has been selected and implemented. The manager must continue to gather information and be prepared to make changes if the problem is not corrected.

WORKSHOP

You and your classmates are managers presented with the following information. The number of employees who are late or absent has increased during the last three months. Discuss how you would respond to the information using the steps in scientific problem solving.

CHECKPOINT

List the steps in scientific problem solving.

_____

_____

THINK CRITICALLY

1. What do you think are the differences between effective and ineffective managers?

_____

_____

2. Why do you think many businesses are reducing the number of managers and instead using employee teams to complete some of the management activities?

_____

_____

_____

3. Do you agree or disagree that supervisors should have a greater span of control than executives?

_____

_____

_____

4. How can managers determine if a situation is a problem or just a symptom of a problem?

_____

_____

_____

MAKING CONNECTIONS

5. **ETHICS** You are a supervisor and have just been told that the company is not doing well. You must lay off one employee from each department. In one department, one employee is a good friend and another you don't like as well. Both have been good employees. If you had to select one of the two people to lose their job, how would you make the decision? How would you deal with your feelings about each person?

_____

_____

_____

6. **BUSINESS MATH** The average manager at Lincoln Associates spends the following hours on management functions: Planning = 16, Organizing = 14, Implementing = 8, Controlling = 6. On average, how many total hours each week do the managers work? What percentage of the workweek does the average manager devote to each management function? Use a computer and spreadsheet software to perform the calculations.

7. **COMMUNICATIONS** Select the management function you think is most important to the successful operation of a business. Using a computer and word processing software, write a two-paragraph memo to your class members identifying the management function and the reasons you chose it.

LESSON 2.2
LEADERSHIP

GOALS

IDENTIFY the characteristics of a good leader

DESCRIBE ways that managers can demonstrate leadership with employees

MANAGERS AS LEADERS

Many employees think that management is an easy job. Most managers do very different work from the people they supervise. Employees may see a manager give directions, evaluate their performance, provide feedback, and solve problems when they occur. When the work is getting done in a department, employees are working well together, and there are no problems, a manager may appear to have little to do. However, those circumstances indicate the manager has done a lot of work in order for things to run smoothly.

One of the most important skills of managers is to work effectively with employees and help them work well together. Employees want to feel a part of the work team and to be involved in deciding how the work will be done.

ON THE $CENE

Some people think there is a generation gap in business today. "Generation X" is used to describe people under 30 years of age who have been entering the workforce in the last decade. They are described as having very different views of work and what they want from their jobs. They are seen as not willing to respond to the types of management used in the past. Do you think that the new generation of workers is different from past generations? If so, how? How can a manager meet the expectations of "Generation X" employees and older employees at the same time?

The most effective managers use leadership to develop effective working relationships. **Leadership** is the ability to influence individuals and groups to cooperatively achieve organizational goals. Leaders have excellent human relations skills. **Human relations** refers to how well people get along with each other when working together. Groups with effective human relations not only get along well with each other but also are more effective in getting work accomplished.

CHARACTERISTICS OF EFFECTIVE LEADERS

Because managers have to rely on others to get most of the work accomplished, leadership skills are very important. Not everyone is a natural leader, but leadership skills can be developed. Because leadership is so important in business, the business may want to hire managers who already have leadership skills. The business also may provide leadership training for employees and managers.

Studies have identified many of the characteristics of effective leaders. Important leadership characteristics are listed below. Those characteristics are personal qualities rather than specific things that leaders do. In fact, two very successful leaders may approach a problem in very different ways and both can be effective. Leaders know how to be flexible and adjust to change.

Important Leadership Characteristics		
Judgment	Objectivity	Initiative
Dependability	Cooperation	Honesty
Courage	Confidence	Stability

HUMAN RELATIONS SKILLS

Managers must be able to work effectively with others. They need to work well with employees, other managers, customers, and everyone who has contact with their department. They also need to insure that employees work well together. With the growing importance of work teams, human relations skills are even more important in business today. Managers need to understand others, communicate effectively, build effective teams, and develop employee job satisfaction.

Understand Others The U.S. workplace has many people from different backgrounds and cultures working together. Managers must recognize this diversity. They also must recognize differences in employee needs, attitudes, and abilities. A manager with effective human relations skills works hard to get to know every employee and to find the best way to work with each one.

Communicate Effectively One of a manager's most important activities is communication. A manager has to communicate with many people using several forms of communication. Those forms include writing, speaking, and listening. Communication in business is both formal and informal. Managers need to understand and use both types appropriately. Managers must understand what information needs to be communicated, when it needs to be communicated, and what communication methods to use.

COMMUNICATE

Managers' use of e-mail is different from employees' use. Managers are more formal and often send letters, reports, and other company documents as e-mail attachments. Employees use e-mail more frequently for informal communications with other employees and with people outside the company. Those communications are sometimes only generally related to the employee's business activities. Do you think companies should restrict the use of e-mail by employees to communications specifically related to the business? Write two paragraphs stating and defending your views.

Build Effective Teams Employees want to feel that they are an important part of the business and of their work group. Team members support each other and offer help to others when needed. People who are part of a team support the goals of the organization and work well together to accomplish the goals. Managers who develop effective teams will have to spend little time closely supervising employee work and solving problems caused by interpersonal conflicts.

Develop Employee Job Satisfaction Employees who are satisfied with their job will want the business to be successful. They will try to do a good job and work well with others. Employees are more likely to be satisfied when the job matches their interests and skills, and when they think their manager will try to help them be successful. When managers demonstrate concern about each employee's job satisfaction, they will get the cooperation and best efforts of those employees.

CHECKPOINT ✓

Why does a manager need effective leadership and human relations skills?

_____

_____

DEMONSTRATE LEADERSHIP

All managers perform the same four functions. However, managers do not all complete their work in the same ways. Their view of employees and how they use power to get work accomplished usually forms the basis for how managers work.

VIEWPOINTS ABOUT EMPLOYEES

Some managers think that employees will not work well unless they are closely supervised. Those managers make most of the decisions and establish rules and procedures for employees to follow. They use rewards for employees who perform well and penalties for those who do not.

Other managers think that employees enjoy their work and put forth their best efforts without a great deal of supervision. They will have fewer work rules and allow employees to take more initiative and make many of the decisions about how work should be done. Managers with this viewpoint will offer praise and encouragement for employees and will work with each employee to solve problems as they develop. They will spend more time on other management activities and less on direct supervision.

Although many managers tend to favor one viewpoint over the other, managers need to be able to adjust the way they work with employees. For example, new employees or those working on tasks they dislike may need more direct supervision. Experienced employees doing work they enjoy will need almost no direction from management. Employees usually prefer managers who appreciate their efforts and are flexible in the type and amount of supervision they give.

USE OF POWER

Managers must be able to influence employees to complete assigned work. They are able to influence others because of the power they hold as managers. Power can be either negative or positive. Managers who force employees to do work because "the manager is the boss" are using *position power*. If they get work done because they control rewards and punishments, they are using *reward power*. Position power and reward power are viewed negatively by employees. They only exist because the person with the power is a manager.

Two other types of power are viewed more positively by employees. A person others look to for help has *expert power*. They are considered leaders because of their expertise. Another type of power is *identity power*. When others look up to a person and want to be accepted by them, they will usually do what the person requests.

Both of these types of power are related to leadership characteristics. If employees respect the manager's expertise or if they want approval or recognition, they will work cooperatively with the manager.

Both employees and managers need leadership skills. When employees are given an assignment, they often will have to work with others to get the work done. Employee teams usually are given the authority to make decisions and manage much of their own work. In each case, the employees will have to demonstrate effective leadership including human relations and the wise use of power.

CHECKPOINT

What are the four types of power managers may use?

_____

_____

_____

but have no authority over line personnel. They are there to help with specialized jobs. Examples of staff positions are legal, information management, strategic planning, and human resource specialists.

Project Organization A newer, more flexible structure is the *project organization.* It combines workers into temporary work teams to complete specific projects. Employees report to a project manager with authority and responsibility for the project. When a new project must be done, employees with the needed skills are assigned to work on the project team. They work for that manager until the project is finished. Then they are assigned to a new project and another project manager. When employees are given new project assignments, managers must be careful to define authority and responsibility, so as not to violate unity of command.

Team Organization The newest type of business organization is known as a team organization. A *team organization* divides employees into permanent work teams. The teams have responsibility and authority for important business activities with limited management control over their daily work. Teams often have team leaders. Team leaders replace the traditional position of supervisor and act as facilitators more than as traditional managers. Rather than solve problems themselves, team leaders help their teams identify problems and work with them to solve the problems as a group. Companies that have developed effective team organizations have a better record of serving customers, reducing absenteeism and turnover, and keeping motivation high.

What are the characteristics of an effective business organization?

_____

_____

INTERNATIONAL BUSINESS METHODS

Doing business in other countries for the first time is challenging for business managers. Several methods make it easier. One method is to use an *import/export business.* This is an independent business with experience in buying and selling products in other countries. A second method is to develop *licensing agreements.* The license gives permission to produce and market the products of the licensing company in another country. Third, *joint ventures* can be created where companies cooperate as full partners to plan and market products and services. Finally, a large company might decide to establish a new division of the company in the country it wants to serve.

THINK CRITICALLY Identify one advantage and one disadvantage for each type of international business method mentioned.

THINK CRITICALLY

1. Do you think strategic or operation planning is more difficult to complete? Why?

_____

_____

_____

2. Why is it important for managers to have employees who work well together? What can managers do to promote good relationships among employees?

_____

_____

_____

_____

3. Why do many businesses continue to use line or line-and-staff organizations rather than project and team organizations?

_____

_____

_____

_____

MAKE CONNECTIONS

4. **COMMUNICATION** An organizational chart is a drawing that shows the structure of an organization, major job classifications, and the reporting relationships among the organization's personnel. Develop a brief oral report that explains how an organizational chart can improve the operations of a business. As a part of the report, find examples of an organizational chart for a business. Write the outline for your report in the lines below.

_____

_____

_____

_____

5. **PSYCHOLOGY** Develop a list of reasons that you think explain why employees are more satisfied and motivated when they are part of a project or team organization than when they are a part of a line or line-and-staff organization. Write a rough draft of your list on the lines below. Then type it using a computer and word processing software.

_____

_____

_____

_____

_____

_____

LESSON 2.4
IMPLEMENT AND CONTROL

GOALS

DESCRIBE implementing activities completed by managers

DISCUSS how controlling activities improve business operations and management

THE IMPLEMENTING FUNCTION

The day-to-day work of a business determines whether the company will be successful or not. If employees are not motivated to do a good job, if time and materials are wasted, or if projects are not completed successfully, problems will quickly develop. It is the responsibility of all managers to make sure the business is operating well.

IMPLEMENTING ACTIVITIES

Implementing involves guiding the work of employees' toward achieving the company's goals. A manager involved in the implementing function may start by communicating with employees about the company's goals and plans. Then the manager and employees may discuss how the needed work will be completed. If needed, training and supervision is provided. The manager must be sure that employees get recognition when they achieve their work

ON THE $CENE

The day couldn't end soon enough for Shami. It was her second week as the new supervisor for her work group. Her group was two days behind schedule on a major project yet most of the employees seemed not to care. Shami had to correct an error today. She got right in the middle of an argument between two employees on who was responsible for the mistake. Tomorrow she will have to begin work on the performance evaluation reports for each employee. She knows that several will not be happy with the results. Shami hopes that management work will get easier with experience. What recommendations do you have to make Shami feel better about her new job?

goals so they remain motivated and committed to doing a good job. To be successful in implementing, managers must be able to communicate, motivate, and encourage teamwork.

Communication Effective communication is more than giving directions. Managers need to listen to employees and involve them in deciding how work should be done. Encouraging employees to contribute their ideas and involving them in deciding the best way to do the work will help gain their respect and commitment.

Motivation Motivation is a set of factors that influence an individual's actions toward accomplishing a goal. There usually is a difference between the goals of a business and the personal goals of each employee. Employees may or may not be motivated to achieve company goals.

Managers don't actually "motivate" employees. Instead they do things to encourage employees to motivate themselves to accomplish company objectives. All people have their own needs. They will choose to do things that will satisfy their needs and avoid doing things that don't. Managers can influence employee performance by understanding individual needs and providing rewards that satisfy those needs when employees accomplish work goals. A reward does not have to be money. People value things like praise, respect, an interesting job assignment, or even a special luncheon or party.

Teamwork Many important jobs in a business require that two or more employees work together. Managers need to be able to develop effective teamwork among the employees they supervise. In most cases, groups can accomplish more than the same number of people working independently.

Even though people work together, they may not be an effective team. People may have misperceptions, biases, or stereotypes about coworkers. They may not have had positive experiences in cooperating to complete a task or know how to make effective team decisions.

Managers can play an important role in developing team effectiveness. They need to understand the characteristics that make groups effective. Then they can help organize the team and make sure everyone understands the expectations for the group. They need to create a work environment that supports teamwork. They also need to help the group resolve problems before they interfere with the group's work and relationships.

OPERATIONS MANAGEMENT

Operations are the major ongoing activities of a business. The operations from one business to another might be very different. For example a manufacturer has product research, product assembly, and shipping as important operations activities. A retailer on the other hand emphasizes merchandising, selling, and customer service. Managers are responsible for the operations of a business. They must work with employees so that the specialized activities required for business operations are performed as planned.

Operations Activities Several activities are part of operations management. Facilities, equipment, materials, and supplies must be available and in good operating condition. Employees must have the knowledge and skills needed to complete their work. Managers must make sure that employees complete their work on schedule and work to resolve problems that could interfere with the successful completion of work.

Managers must be prepared to implement the activities assigned to their area of responsibility. Some activities are common to almost all managers. For example, most managers must hire new employees, monitor work schedules, and communicate policies and procedures. However, each manager also is responsible for the specialized operations of the work unit. For example, the information systems manager must insure that computer systems are operational, the company's Internet sites are up-to-date, and that software is problem-free.

Improving Quality Companies must operate efficiently to keep costs low, so that they can compete successfully. At the same time, customers are demanding improved quality but don't think they should have to spend a great deal more money for that quality. Those pressures have caused businesses to pay a great deal of attention to how work is accomplished in order to improve quality while controlling costs.

The efforts to increase the effectiveness and efficiency of specific business operations are known as **process improvement**. Procedures have been developed to help managers and employees identify quality problems and make improvements in the way work is completed. Companies that implement process improvement efforts usually see positive results in customer satisfaction, sales, and profits.

CHECKPOINT

What are several day-to-day activities managers complete as a part of the implementing function?

_____

_____

CONTROLLING BUSINESS OPERATIONS

E ach of the functions of management is important and related to all other functions. Planning sets the direction for the work of the business. Managers must organize the business to be able to implement the plans that were made. The day-to-day activities of the business must be implemented in order for the plans to be realized. The last activity, controlling, determines if the plans have been accomplished and the goals of the business achieved. Controlling is used to identify successes and problems in order to improve business operations.

THE CONTROLLING PROCESS

Controlling involves three basic steps.

1. Establishing standards for each of the company's goals.

2. Measuring and comparing performance against the established standards to see if performance met the goals.

3. Taking corrective action when performance falls short of the standards.

Example The following example illustrates the process. A cell phone manufacturer has an order for 1,000 telephones that must be ready for shipment in eight days. To meet the goal, a standard is set to produce 125 cell phones each day. At the end of two days, only 130 cell phones had been completed. The standard was to produce 250 cell phones in two days. Subtracting 130 from 250 gives 120 phones. Because production is 120 fewer than needed to meet the standard, the manager must take action to produce even more telephones during the remaining six days. The corrective  action may include scheduling overtime work or assigning more employees to the production unit. The manager also needs to study the manufacturing process to see why the standard that was originally set could not be met.

Possible Actions When performance is not meeting the standard, managers can take three possible actions.

1. Take steps to improve performance

2. Change policies and procedures

3. Revise the standard

Typically, if planning has been done carefully, standards should not be changed. In the example, the company cannot just reduce the number of phones produced because it would be unable to fill the order. The company should know from past experience whether producing 125 phones a day could be accomplished. Only under unusual circumstances, such as inability to obtain needed materials or major equipment failure, would the standard be reduced.

TYPES OF STANDARDS

Controlling cannot occur without goals and standards. Managers set standards as a part of planning. The standards need to be established carefully because they will be used to determine how work will be accomplished. Standards should be achievable but stretch employees to do their best. The major types of standards are quantity, quality, time, and cost standards.

Quantity Standards Quantity standards establish how much work is expected to be performed. Production managers may specify the minimum number of units to be produced each hour, day, or month by individual employees or work teams. Sales managers may establish the number of prospective customers that sales representatives must contact daily or weekly or the number of orders that should be placed in a specific time period.

THE COMPUTER BECOMES A MANAGER Controlling activities can take a great deal of a manager's time. Computer programs are now being developed that can do much of the controlling work and allow the manager to concentrate on the most important problems. A computer can track how much time it is taking to complete a task and signal when an activity is behind schedule. Computers monitor the production of delicate equipment. If a part does not meet the precise size or shape required, the computer will stop production until a correction is made. A computer can even identify when an employee is not performing a task in the way it should be done. If a mechanic completing auto repairs does not follow the appropriate procedure, a reminder of the correct procedure will appear on the computer screen. With computers being used to monitor work, managers can be sure that everything is working well unless the computer indicates otherwise.

THINK CRITICALLY In what types of work do you think computers would be most effective in handling the controlling function? Do you think that computers can perform the controlling function for every type of work? Why or why not?

WORKSHOP

A local charity has asked your class to use a computer publishing program to design and print its monthly newsletter. They will pay $1.25 per copy you produce. Your class wants to make sure you are able to make money and produce a quality newsletter. Prepare a time, quantity, quality, and cost standard your class will use to control the newsletter production.

Quality Standards Most work must meet a quality standard. Perfection—having no errors—may be the only acceptable standard for some products and services. However for some activities, quality standards allow for some variance. For example, when sewing seams on a pair of slacks, the standard allows for 1/16 of an inch difference in the size of the seam.

Time Standards The amount of time it takes to complete an activity has an effect on costs, the quantity of work completed, and often on the quality of the work. Time standards are very important to some businesses such as airlines, television stations, newspapers, and theaters. If they do not meet their schedules, they suffer an immediate financial loss. Failure to maintain time standards may not be as obvious in other businesses but can affect the number of products produced and how related activities are scheduled.

Cost Standards Controlling costs is very important to most businesses. When costs increase, profits usually go down. Budgets are the most frequently used tool to control costs. They are used to establish cost standards. A budget is prepared as a part of planning and then becomes a controlling tool. Managers collect cost information on a regular basis and compare it to budgeted amounts. If costs exceed the budget, corrective action should be considered. That can include finding ways to reduce costs or increase the amount of income for the business to cover the increased costs.

CHECKPOINT ✓

What are the four types of standards used in controlling?

_____

_____

_____

THINK CRITICALLY

1. Why is the implementing function the most important management activity for supervisors and most employees?

_____

_____

_____

_____

2. What are some ways that managers can motivate employees without increasing their pay or benefits?

_____

_____

_____

3. Compare the types of operations management activities that would be needed in a manufacturing business with those needed in a service business.

_____

_____

_____

_____

4. The word "evaluating" is sometimes used instead of "controlling" to describe the fourth management function. In your view, which of the terms best describes that function? Why?

_____

_____

_____

MAKE CONNECTIONS

5. **TECHNOLOGY** Use the Internet to find information on effective team-work. Prepare a list of three things team members should do to make sure the team is effective.

_____

_____

_____

6. **COMMUNICATIONS** You are the manager of the work group responsi-ble for manufacturing the cell phones discussed in the lesson. Because production is below standard, you have to schedule all employees to work three hours of overtime each day for the next six days. You know many already have made plans, so they will not be happy with the increased work hours. Plan what you will say to the employees during a group meeting to explain the required overtime work. Remember that the way they feel after you meet with them will affect the way they perform their work. Present your speech to a group of classmates.

CHAPTER SUMMARY

LESSON 2.1 The Manager's Role

A. The primary work of all managers can be grouped within four functions, including planning, organizing, implementing, and controlling.

B. Employees want to be involved in decision making and considered an important part of the business.

LESSON 2.2 Leadership

A. One of the most important skills of managers is to work effectively with employees and help employees work well together.

B. If employees respect their manager's expertise or if they want approval or recognition, they will work cooperatively with the manager.

LESSON 2.3 Plan and Organize

A. Without careful planning, the business will not have direction and managers and employees will not know what to do.

B. The division of work, workflow, and employee relationships must be considered to make sure the business is well organized.

LESSON 2.4 Implement and Control

A. The day-to-day work of a business determines whether the company will be successful or not. It is the responsibility of all managers to make sure the business is operating well.

B. Controlling involves three basic steps, including establishing standards, measuring and comparing performance, and taking corrective action.

VOCABULARY BUILDER

Choose the term that best fits the definition. Write the letter of the answer in the space provided. Some terms may not be used.

_____ **1.** Determining how plans can be accomplished most effectively and arranging resources to complete work

_____ **2.** The ability to influence individuals and groups to cooperatively achieve organizational goals

_____ **3.** Specific and set direction for one part of the business for a short period of time

_____ **4.** Broad and general direction for the entire business for a long period of time

_____ **5.** Carrying out the plans and helping employees to work effectively

_____ **6.** The major ongoing activities of a business

_____ **7.** Efforts to increase the effectiveness and efficiency of specific business operations

_____ **8.** The process of accomplishing the goals of an organization through the effective use of people and other resources

a. controlling

b. human relations

c. implementing

d. leadership

e. management

f. operation plans

g. operations

h. organizing

i. planning

j. process improvement

k. strategic plans

REVIEW CONCEPTS

9. What are the four functions that describe the work of managers?

_____

_____

10. How is the work of a supervisor different from the work of a top executive?

_____

_____

_____

11. What are the key human relations skills needed by leaders?

_____

_____

12. Identify and differentiate among the four types of power.

_____

_____

_____

13. Why is planning considered the most important management function?

_____

_____

_____

_____

14. What are the important factors that should be considered to make sure the business is well organized?

_____

_____

_____

15. How can people work together and still not be an effective team?

_____

_____

_____

16. What are the three basic steps in controlling?

_____

_____

_____

POINT YOUR BROWSER

b2000.swep.com

REVIEW

APPLY WHAT YOU LEARNED

17. Describe one specific management activity for each of the four management functions.

_____

_____

_____

_____

18. Do you think some people are natural leaders or do they learn to be leaders based on their experiences?

_____

_____

_____

_____

19. Why are companies increasingly using project and team organization structures rather than line or line-and-staff structures?

_____

_____

_____

20. Is it possible for a business to keep costs low and quality high at the same time? Why or why not?

_____

_____

_____

21. You just purchased a pizza shop near a college campus and are beginning to plan your operations. Develop one policy, one procedure, and one standard you will use in operating this business.

_____

_____

_____

_____

22. Which of the management functions do you think is most important to the success of a business and why?

_____

_____

_____

_____

CHAPTER 2

MAKE CONNECTIONS

23. SCIENCE Business managers use the same process for decision making as scientists. The steps in scientific problem solving are (1) identify the problem, (2) list possible solutions, (3) carefully analyze the possible solutions, and (4) select the best solution using the results of the analysis. A manager of a video rental store is having problems with customers who don't rewind their videos before returning them. Use the scientific problem solving process to develop a solution for the business. Present your solution in class.

24. BUSINESS MATH A survey was completed with 300 managers and 500 employees. Each was asked which of the four types of power would be most effective with beginning employees. The answers are shown in the table below. Complete the table by calculating the percentage of total responses for each group. Then determine the difference in the percentages between the two groups for each type of power. If available, use spreadsheet software to do your calculations.

Type of power	Supervisor responses	Percent	Employee responses	Percent	Difference
Position	88	____	52	10.4	_____
Reward	102	____	125	25.0	_____
Expert	65	____	180	36.0	_____
Identity	45	____	143	28.6	_____

25. JOURNALISM Identify a person who has been a successful manager for several years. The person can be a friend or family member or someone you don't know well. Prepare at least three interview questions in advance of meeting with the person to learn how they prepared to become a manager and the types of knowledge and skills they use in their role as a manager. Using a computer and word processing software, write a newspaper article complete with a headline using the information from the interview. Use the lines below to develop questions for your interview.

_____

_____

_____

_____

26. TECHNOLOGY The Internet now allows managers to develop work teams without having to bring people together face-to-face. Several people can work together using a computer, modem, video camera, and an Internet browser. Join with a group of other students to brainstorm a list of advantages and disadvantages of a "virtual" work team compared to a traditional "face-to-face" team. Find information on the Internet and use library resources such as business books and magazines that describe the characteristics of entrepreneurs and managers. Compare that information with the lists your group developed.

COMMUNICATION AND INFORMATION SYSTEMS

LESSONS

3.1 BUSINESS COMMUNICATION

3.2 WRITTEN AND ORAL COMMUNICATION

3.3 INFORMATION TECHNOLOGY

CAREERS IN BUSINESS

DOW JONES & CO.

Dow Jones, headquartered in New York, NY, has been a publisher of business information since 1882. Its premier business newspaper, *The Wall Street Journal,* is read daily by nearly 2 billion people worldwide. It also publishes *The Asian Wall Street Journal, The Wall Street Journal Europe,* and Latin America's *AméricaEconomía.*

Dow Jones has moved into the Internet with its online edition, WSJ.com, and Dow Jones news and research services. It provides business content for programs on CNBC, a cable television channel that it co-owns.

A Copywriter/Marketing Coordinator for Dow Jones' publications needs two or more years of experience in consumer marketing. Publication experience also is helpful. Strong writing and interpersonal skills are essential. A newer position is Interactive Moderator and Producer for WSJ.com. This person hosts online live chats with guest experts as well as managing bulletin board discussions. A bachelor's degree is required along with computer knowledge and excellent news judgment.

THINK CRITICALLY

1. Why is it important to offer business information through newspapers, cable television, and the Internet?
2. Which of the two positions described most appeal to you, and why?

PROJECT

Improve Business Communication

PROJECT OBJECTIVES

- Identify the business needs for communication and the major forms used
- Describe skills needed for communication in business
- Recommend ways that business communication can be improved

GETTING STARTED

Read through the Project Process below. Make a list of materials and information you will need. Decide how you will get the needed materials or information.

PROJECT PROCESS

Part 1 **LESSON 3.1** Work in small groups to develop two lists. List one will describe the types of communication needed inside a business. List two will describe the types of communication a business exchanges with outside parties. Identify the types of media that are most often used for communication inside and outside of businesses.

Part 2 **LESSON 3.2** Write brief descriptions of communication skills employees and managers need. Base your descriptions on interviews you conduct with people who are employees or managers in business.

Part 3 **LESSON 3.3** In your groups, brainstorm as many types of communication technology you can think of that businesspeople use. Brainstorm specific examples, such as voice mail, computer, or personal digital assistant. Review each type of technology and discuss how the technology has helped to improve business communication.

CHAPTER REVIEW

Project Wrap-up You have been hired as a communication consultant for a mail-order business. Using the information from the other parts of this project, prepare a two-page written report to the business's managers that discusses ways they can improve communications with their employees and customers.

LESSON 3.1
BUSINESS COMMUNICATION

GOALS

UNDERSTAND the simple communication model

DESCRIBE several types of business communications and how they are used

EFFECTIVE COMMUNICATION

Studies have shown that, on average, managers spend as much as two-thirds of each day communicating. Managers use many forms of communication. They talk directly to employees or other managers and call customers and colleagues from other businesses. They write memos, letters, and reports and exchange many e-mail messages. When participating in meetings managers listen, discuss, and even express their feelings with facial expressions and body language. When you consider all of the ways managers communicate, you can understand why their day is filled by communications activities.

UNDERSTAND COMMUNICATION

Communication is the exchange of information between two or more people in a way that results in common understanding. Communication is much more than someone providing information to others. It is a two-way process

ON THE $CENE

MariLee Masone has been the manager of a call center for the Conley Co. for three years. She believes in open and clear communication with all employees. MariLee has just been told that the third shift of her call center is going to be eliminated. She has been promised that the company will try to keep all employees, but they will have to work different hours. About one-third of her staff will be asked to move to a new call center being opened on the other side of the city, about 25 miles away. MariLee is aware that rumors are already spreading about the change. How should MariLee explain the change to employees? How can she handle the rumors that she knows are untrue or only partially true?

BUSINESS MATH CONNECTION

Research has shown that in a typical day, managers spend the following hours on certain activities. Rank the activities from most time taken to least time. Which one activity takes the most time? Which activity takes the least time? How many hours do managers typically spend in a day on communication activities?

Listening	2.5 h	Writing	0.5 h	Other activities	2.5 h
Reading	1.0 h	Speaking	1.5 h		

SOLUTION

Activity ranks from most to least:

Listening 2.5 h, Other 2.5 h, Speaking 1.5 h, Reading 1.0 h, Writing 0.5 h

Listening takes the most time and writing takes the least time.
Total time spent on communication activities:

Listening + Speaking + Reading + Writing = Total
2.5   +   1.5   +   1.0   +   0.5   = 5.5 hours

Managers typically spend 5.5 hours per day on communication activities.

---

between a **sender,** the person or organization providing the information, and the **receiver,** one or more people with whom the sender wants to communicate. Receivers can send feedback to the sender indicating whether they understand the message or not, ask questions, or provide additional information. Communication is more than words and information. Communication can occur through sounds, pictures, body language, facial expression, and many other ways.

A Simple Communication Model

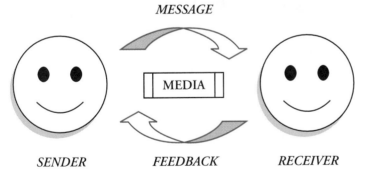

MESSAGE

MEDIA

SENDER   *FEEDBACK*   *RECEIVER*

Communication occurs through **media** that are the methods used to move information between senders and receivers. Common communication media in business are telephones, e-mail, letters, reports, and face-to-face. There are many other media types available for communications as well.

COMMUNICATION PROBLEMS

Communication problems can occur for many reasons. One of the most important occurs when the sender doesn't understand the receiver or is

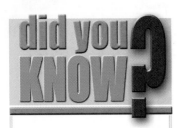

unconcerned about whether the receiver understands the message. Both the sender and receiver have responsibilities for effective communication. The sender needs to use communication methods and language familiar to the receiver. The receiver must let the sender know if the message is not clear.

Communication problems are likely to occur due to distractions around the sender or receiver. Distractions can include noise, interruptions, other communication occurring at the same time, or lack of concentration. People need to try to reduce or remove possible distractions when communicating.

Effective communication may be more difficult when senders and receivers have different experiences or backgrounds such as age, culture, or education level. Those differences cause people to apply different meaning to information. For example, when a parent says, "be home early" to a child, the parent may be thinking 9 P.M. while the child is thinking 10:30 P.M.

Technical problems with media also interfere with communication. A power failure may result in lost e-mail messages. A poor connection between cell phones increases the likelihood that some of the conversation will not be heard. For important communications, media should be selected that are reliable and that both sender and receiver are comfortable using.

CHECKPOINT

What are the elements in a simple communication model?

_____

_____

COMMUNICATE IN BUSINESS

Businesspeople depend on others for success. Managers rely on employees to complete the daily work of a business. Members of a work team depend on each other to successfully complete a project. The business must attract and satisfy customers in order to sell its products and make a profit. Each of those relationships requires effective communication.

Internal or External Communication *Internal communication* occurs between people within the business. *External communication* is information exchanged by people in the business with others outside the business. External communication occurs with customers, vendors, and others. Some internal communications are *horizontal,* that is, communication between people at the same level of an organization. Others are *vertical,* or communications that cross organizational levels. If several supervisors hold a meeting to discuss a common project, they are using horizontal communication. If the chief executive of a company sends a letter to all employees, the executive is using vertical communication.

Formal or Informal Communication *Formal communication* includes the ways that have been organized for people to communicate in the business. Most businesses have rules and policies that identify how people should communicate in specific situations or what is considered appropriate or inappropriate communication. Companies invest money in technologies such as computers, fax machines, and telephones to support formal communication. *Informal communication* refers to the unofficial ways information is exchanged in business. It is often completed face-to-face or by telephone. E-mail also is a popular means of informal communication.

The informal way most information moves through a business is often called the *grapevine.* Information exchanged in this way may become distorted or inaccurate. Employees share information informally both during the work day and away from work. That communication is important to people and often contributes to positive working relationships. Managers cannot and should not try to prevent informal communication as long as it is positive and not harmful. However, managers should be aware of informal communication and attempt to correct inaccurate information.

As a class, discuss how a manager should use effective communications in the following situation. The manager must respond to a customer's letter complaining about the quality of customer service she received when she tried to return a product and get a refund.

IMPROVE BUSINESS COMMUNICATION

Because communication is so important in business, managers need to have effective communication skills. That includes the ability to speak, listen, read, and write well. In addition, managers can improve communications by carefully planning, sending, and receiving them. Here are some tips.

1. *Understand the receiver.* To make sure that messages will be understood, the sender needs to identify who will be the receiver and how to most effectively communicate with that person. The receiver's experience, culture, language, and attitudes about the subject of the message will affect the way the message is understood.

2. *Carefully plan the message.* Determine what needs to be communicated. Remove any unnecessary information and use words and images that will be understood by the receiver. Provide reasons or explanations that help the receiver accept and feel positive about the message.

3. *Choose the best media.* Usually the sender has choices in how to communicate. A message can be delivered in person, by telephone, in a letter, or in an e-mail. Some media are better suited for certain messages.

4. *Follow up on all communications.* If a message is important enough to send, you should make sure the information is received and understood. When you talk to people, listen to their responses and observe their body language to determine if the information was understood. The sender should ask the receiver for feedback or check to make sure the person took appropriate action in response to the message.

CHECKPOINT ✓

What are the common types of communication in business?

_____

_____

THINK CRITICALLY

1. Why is it important for managers to spend most of their time each day communicating?

_____

_____

_____

2. What are possible types of distractions that could interfere with effective communication if a manager is trying to hold a meeting with 15 employees?

_____

_____

_____

3. Why should a manager avoid trying to discourage an employee grapevine?

_____

_____

_____

4. How can the lack of understanding of the receiver interfere with effective communication?

_____

_____

_____

MAKE CONNECTIONS

5. BUSINESS MATH Use the information from the Business Math Connection on page 59 on how a manager spends an average day. Using spreadsheet software, prepare a pie chart illustrating the percentage of time spent on each activity listed.

6. DEBATE Work with a group of students to take a position and debate the following topic.

Effective internal communications is more important to the success of a business than effective external communications.

Use the following lines to take notes as you prepare your position.

_____

_____

_____

_____

_____

_____

_____

LESSON 3.2
WRITTEN AND ORAL COMMUNICATION

GOALS

IDENTIFY common forms of written and oral communication

DESCRIBE how to improve writing, speaking, and listening skills

FORMS OF COMMUNICATION

Communication can make the difference in whether a business is successful or not. Employees may have the needed skills to do their work well. However, if they don't understand what needs to be done or misunderstand directions from their manager, they will not be effective. If customers cannot obtain the information they need or if they think employees are not sincere in handling their problems, they will take their business to another company. Ineffective communications can lead to misunderstandings, poor work relationships, work errors, dissatisfied customers, and lost sales.

Managers face many situations in which they must communicate in order to accomplish the work of the business. Effective managers are effective

ON THE $CENE

Frank Young had scheduled a meeting with the people in his department to discuss the change to a new e-mail program. Five of the 15 employees were unable to attend the meeting due to conflicting activities. Those who did attend seemed to understand the procedures to be followed in changing to the new system and asked very few questions. Today, only one day after the new system was in place, Frank had to spend most of this time handling employee complaints, answering questions that were covered in the meeting, and helping most of the employees begin using the new e-mail program. Why does it seem the meeting was not effective? Was there a better way for Frank to provide the needed information?

communicators. There are many ways managers communicate. The two common forms of business communication are written and oral communication. **Written communication** uses text and images to convey information. **Oral communication** is the use of spoken words, body language, and listening to convey information. Neither written nor oral communication is effective unless there is understanding of the information and appropriate action is taken by the receivers of the message.

WRITTEN COMMUNICATION

Much of the formal communication in business is completed in writing. Business letters, memos, and reports are used regularly for both internal and external communication. Written communications are used in business because much of the information communicated is complex and detailed. It is also used to provide a record of the information sent from one person to others. A third reason for using written communication is because information needs to be provided to a large number of people in a way that communicates accurately, quickly, and at a low cost.

Business Reports   The most complex form of written communication in business is the business report. A report provides detailed information on a problem, question, or business project. Many reports contain both text and graphics. Common graphics used in reports are tables, graphs, and charts which are used to illustrate and highlight important information.

Business reports are often 50 to 100 pages or longer. They may take several days or weeks to prepare, and are written after careful study of an issue. For example, a business may want to decide whether a new product idea will be accepted by customers or how to reduce the time and cost of distributing products. The manager responsible may work with a team of people to study the issue, consider alternative solutions, and then prepare a report. Executives, who will be responsible for a final decision, will review the report.

Business Letters   Traditionally, business letters have been the primary method of formal, written communication in business. More than 100 million business letters are mailed each day. Business letters are used to communicate a limited amount of specific information to one person or an identified group of people. Most business letters are written on the letterhead of the company and use a professional format that includes the following.

■ Date

■ Inside address—the name, business title, and business address of the recipient

■ Salutation—formal greeting such as "Dear Ms. Slavin"

■ Body—the message of the letter in paragraph form

■ Complimentary close—a formal ending such as "Sincerely yours"

■ Signature

■ Sender's name and business title

Memos   Business memos are a shorter, less formal means of written communication. Memos are frequently used for written communications within a company, especially among people who know each other. Managers use memos to answer a specific question, to provide instructions or urgent information, or to recognize or acknowledge the work of employees. They also use memos for regular, brief communications with other managers.

Memos should contain a limited amount of information. They usually are a page or less in length and frequently only two or three paragraphs long. Most memos use a standard format that lists the recipients' and sender's names, the date, and the subject of the memo. Businesses often have a standard memo form employees can use. While the sender always signs business letters, memos may not include a signature.

E-mail Today e-mail has become a popular form of both business and personal communication. E-mail is convenient, quick, and easy to use. There is no need to print the e-mail message unless either the sender or recipient wants a permanent record of the communication.

E-mail is considered an informal method of communication. It does not convey the professional image of a business letter. E-mail should be used carefully. There are many examples of e-mail messages sent in haste or anger that the sender later wishes had not been sent. Some people do not take time to write an e-mail message so that it clearly communicates the desired information. There also is a tendency to be less concerned about grammar and spelling in e-mail messages. This can give a very poor impression of the business and the person sending the message.

Tips for Effective Business E-Mail

- Construct an e-mail message like a business memo.

- Choose to send e-mail when written communication is important and it is clear a letter or memo is not needed.

- Use a simple, direct subject line that communicates the primary purpose or content.

- Plan the message to get and keep the reader's attention and to specifically communicate the necessary information.

- Write the message using clear, professional language.

- Use proper spelling and punctuation, including the use of paragraphs.

- Do not send e-mail in haste, anger, or for inappropriate messages.

- Carefully select the recipients to be sure each needs to know the information included.

- Do not forward business e-mail messages received from others without the approval of the sender.

ORAL COMMUNICATION

Managers need effective oral communication skills as well as written skills. When asked to identify the common types of oral communication in business, most people think of personalized, one-to-one interactions. Common examples include a salesperson talking with a customer, a receptionist answering a telephone, a manager discussing job procedures or work performance with an employee, and an executive calling a colleague in another business.

In small groups, gather information on how to conduct an effective meeting. Then prepare an agenda for a short meeting and complete a demonstration of an effective meeting for the other members of your class.

Each of these situations is important, but there are many others. In addition to those person-to-person examples, other types of oral communication used in business are speeches and presentations, meetings, and group discussions.

While written communication is limited to text and graphics, oral communication includes the spoken words of the sender and receiver, the listening skills of each, body language that often conveys a great deal of meaning, and even visual materials used by the sender as a part of the information presented. The words chosen, the speed and volume of speech, the length of the presentation or conversation, and even the physical and emotional feelings of the sender or receiver can influence the effectiveness of the message.

Speeches and Presentations The most formal types of oral communication are speeches and presentations. Executives or people who have special knowledge or expertise to be shared with an audience typically give speeches. Speeches often are delivered to very large groups of people in a short period of time, from 15 to 45 minutes. While some speakers use slides or other visual aids, many use only words to communicate. That means the words must be carefully chosen, the speech well organized, and the speaker's delivery prepared and rehearsed.

Presentations are a combination of written information, graphics, and a speech or discussion. Presentations are used to present new and often complex information, to provide training, or to help a group plan an activity or solve a problem. They often include a question-and-answer or discussion period. Just as with speeches, presentations must be carefully planned and the presenter, well prepared. In addition, visual aids such as handouts, slides, or materials projected from a computer should be developed to emphasize important points, help explain complex topics, or aid the audience in remembering the information.

Meetings The situation when a few people come together to address specific business issues is a **meeting**. Meetings can be informational, problem solving, or a combination of both. Many meetings are ineffective because they are unfocused and unstructured. Managers should hold meetings when there is a clear purpose, develop an agenda and time schedule for the meeting, and make sure all participants have that information before attending. Most meetings should involve everyone who attends rather than having most people sit and listen to reports or discussion by a very few people.

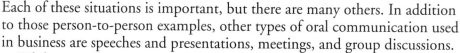

CHECKPOINT

List four types of written communications and at least three types of oral communications used in business.

_____

_____

_____

DEVELOP COMMUNICATION SKILLS

One of the most important sets of skills that you can develop if you want to become a business manager is effective communication. When you consider the types of communication that managers use and the amount of time spent communicating each day, you recognize why people with those skills will have an advantage when competing for management positions. You should develop writing, reading, speaking, and listening skills and be comfortable with a variety of formal and informal communication methods.

IMPROVE WRITING SKILLS

Managers regularly use both formal and informal written communications. Whether drafting a formal letter to a customer in response to a complaint, sending a memo of thanks to employees for extra effort on a project, or writing an item for the company newsletter explaining a new policy, the ability to communicate effectively in writing is an important skill.

Effective writing begins with an understanding of grammar, sentence and paragraph structure, and spelling. Even though word processing programs offer assistance in spell checking and word usage, that is not a substitute for the personal responsibility of the writer. Misspellings and incorrect word usage easily distract readers and create a negative impression of the writer.

Considering the reader's viewpoint helps the writer develop a written message that the recipient will understand and view in a positive way. Some people think that business correspondence should be very formal, impersonal, and use words that are not a part of most peoples' daily language. That is not the case and will only result in miscommunication.

Any written communication should begin by focusing on the purpose of the communication. It should use language that establishes a positive tone.

COMMUNICATE ACROSS CULTURES

Many managers will be given international assignments during their careers or will be responsible for managing employees from other countries and cultures. Awareness of cultural communication differences is important in order to avoid misunderstandings and uncomfortable situations. Consider the following examples. If an American scratches his or her head, it usually means "I don't understand." In Japan, it means "I'm angry." Americans may nod their head to indicate agreement, while people from some African countries pound one fist into the other open palm, and people from Middle Eastern cultures clasp their hands and point their forefingers toward the speaker.

THINK CRITICALLY Are you aware of other cultural communication differences? How can you become aware of those differences among the people with whom you work?

If the reader is upset or angered, it will be difficult to remain objective. The communication should end with a clear summary or by identifying an action.

IMPROVE SPEAKING SKILLS

Most managers will be called upon regularly to deliver speeches, lead discussions, or make presentations. Public speaking ability is an important communication skill. Effective speaking results from careful preparation, practice, and confidence. Even when meeting informally with employees, it is important to plan and make notes of important information to be communicated.

Planning a speech or presentation begins by identifying the audience and the purpose of the presentation. The speaker's words, examples, and presentation style must match the audience for effective communications. The purpose can be determined by asking, "What does the audience need to know?" and "What is the audience expected to do with the information?"

Each speech or presentation should be developed using an outline of key points. The preparation may include developing examples to explain important or complicated points. Many people prepare visual aids to focus the audience's attention and to reinforce key points. Many speakers prepare a complete "script" to be sure they include all information. It can be practiced so the speaker does not appear to be reading from the script. Include opportunities for the audience to participate in the presentation or to ask questions during or at the end of the speech. As with written communications, a specific, well-organized summary is essential.

IMPROVE LISTENING SKILLS

Effective communication requires understanding between the sender and receiver. *Active listening* is an important skill for both the receiver and the sender. The receiver needs to listen carefully to the message of the sender, and the sender must listen carefully to the feedback provided by the receiver. Active listening involves four steps.

1. Eliminate any distractions that can interfere with hearing.

2. Focus attention on the speaker and concentrate on the message.

3. Listen to the entire message and avoid making premature judgements.

4. Ask questions to be sure you understand the message.

Communication is more than words. Meaning also is conveyed through body language and tone of voice. The background and experience of the speaker will affect the meaning of the message. An active listener must try to understand the speaker as well as the message for effective communication.

What are the four steps involved in active listening?

_____

_____

THINK CRITICALLY

1. Why must effective managers be effective communicators?

_____

_____

_____

2. Do you believe the level of management affects the amount and type of oral and written communications used by managers?

_____

_____

_____

3. What are some common communication problems that lead to ineffective meetings?

_____

_____

_____

4. What are some ways that managers can improve their writing, speaking, and listening skills?

_____

_____

_____

MAKE CONNECTIONS

5. WRITING A customer has written to you complaining that she ordered a gift from your company for her daughter's birthday, but it arrived five days late. Using a computer and word processing software, write a one-page letter to the customer offering a solution and creating a positive image of your company.

6. SPEECH Prepare a three to five minute speech on the importance of effective communication in business. Prepare at least one visual aid for your speech. Practice the speech and then present it to a group of classmates. Use the following lines to write the outline for your speech.

_____

_____

_____

_____

_____

_____

_____

_____

LESSON 3.3
INFORMATION TECHNOLOGY

DESCRIBE how technology can improve business communication

IDENTIFY the parts of an information management system and how it is used in business

TECHNOLOGY IN BUSINESS

Computers were introduced in business in the last century. They have become more and more important each year. Desktop and laptop computers are now a part of the daily work activities of many employees. Computers also are used to monitor and control machines and work activities in factories, warehouses, and offices.

The effective use of technology has allowed workers to become more productive and businesses to become more efficient. Because computers have received a great deal of attention in business, it is easy to believe that technology in business has to involve the use of computers. However, technology has

ON THE $CENE

Oren Warner is a manager on the cutting edge of technology. She has used a desktop computer and the Internet for many years. Almost all of her correspondence is sent via e-mail or electronic file exchange. She maintains budgets and department records using spreadsheet and database software. She uses a statistics package to analyze information and a graphics package to summarize information. Oren travels with a laptop computer, a cell phone, and a personal digital assistant that have wireless connections to the Internet. Other managers ask her how she has time to develop the skills necessary to use all of the technology. Ms. Warner says, "I estimate that the technology saves me at least 2 1/2 hours a day in communication and information management, and it definitely makes me a better manager." In what ways do you believe using technology saves time for managers? How can it actually improve management in a business?

been an important part of businesses for many years before computers were invented. A basic definition of **technology** is the practical application of science and engineering. Based on that definition, anything that improves equipment, materials, and work processes that results from scientific study and research is considered technology. The first widespread use of assembly lines by Henry Ford is an example of technology, as is the development and use of robots to replace humans in tedious or dangerous work. A tool that has been redesigned to be used more safely or more quickly is an example of improved technology.

COMMUNICATION TECHNOLOGY

In addition to the many other uses, technology is used to improve communication in business. Improved office equipment, copy and fax machines, telephone systems, and information storage systems are examples of those improvements. Especially in the last two decades, computers have played an important role in improving business communications. Personal computers and word processors have replaced typewriters, and data processing software and electronic spreadsheets have aided bookkeepers and accountants in recording information for financial records and reports.

The Internet and e-mail make it possible for information and messages to be sent almost instantaneously from business to business and person to person. Letters and other mail delivered by the U.S. Postal Service and similar organizations are now referred to as *snail mail*, meaning mail that must be physically handled resulting in a longer delivery time.

DIGITAL SIGNATURES One issue that has prevented the increased use of the Internet for business correspondence is the requirement for signatures on many documents in order for them to be legal. Most people are willing to accept a letter or memo sent via e-mail that contains the printed name of the sender and no written signature. However until recently that practice has not been acceptable for legal documents.

In 2000, the U.S. Congress passed the Millennium Digital Commerce Act that makes "digital" signatures legal. Businesses and government are working together to develop a process to create *digital signatures.* A digital signature is a unique electronically coded identifier that is attached to a document to be sent using the Internet or e-mail. While it will not look like a handwritten signature, it is accepted as an official, legal identification for the person sending the document.

THINK CRITICALLY What kinds of security procedures can be developed to insure that the digital signature is authentic?

CHOOSE TECHNOLOGY

Selecting the communication technology to be used is not easy for managers. New technology is expensive and employees often resist using new equip-

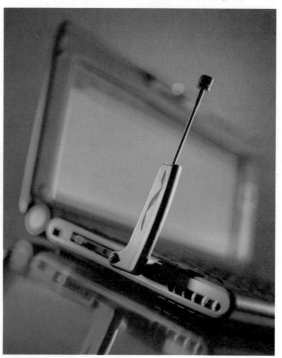

ment and procedures. Changes in technology also require time and money to train employees to use the new technology. When the new equipment is first used, work will likely be slower, and there will be more errors until employees become more comfortable with it.

At one time, it was believed that new technology would replace many employees in a business and result in fewer errors and reduced costs. However, experience has shown that while technology may eliminate some low-skilled employees, it requires the business to hire other high-skilled employees to maintain the new equipment. Experience also has shown that costs and work errors are not always lower with the use of technology.

When making decisions to use new communication technology, managers should ask the following questions.

1. Is the company experiencing communications problems that can be solved with the new technology?

2. How certain are we that the new technology will improve communications if implemented successfully?

3. Will the cost of the technology and the necessary training be less than the resulting improvement in business operations?

4. Is the business committed to training employees, customers, and others who must use the technology so it will be accepted and used effectively?

WORKSHOP

Review magazines and newspapers to identify new types of communication technology being used by businesses. For each technology identified, describe how it will improve communications. Also point out possible problems that might result from its use in a company.

CHECKPOINT

What are some examples of technology that are used in business to improve communications?

_____

_____

_____

USE OF INFORMATION IN BUSINESS

Managers and other employees need information in order to make decisions and run a business. But they face several problems. A great deal of information is available in businesses. However, much of it is not helpful for a specific decision and some of it may not be accurate. There are many sources of information, but some sources are not easy to access. Managers have a limited amount of time to make decisions and a large amount of information to review. Finally when a decision is made, the people affected often want to know what information was used to make the decision.

MANAGEMENT INFORMATION SYSTEMS

Companies have developed information management systems to assist managers with those problems. An **information management system** is a comprehensive process for obtaining, organizing, storing, and providing information to improve decision-making in an organization. An information management system is made up of five components as shown below.

Information Management System

| RAW DATA | INPUT | ANALYSIS/ STORAGE | OUTPUT | MANAGEMENT INFORMATION |

Raw data are all of the needed facts, figures, and other information generated in and outside of a business. *Analysis/storage* is the technology used to maintain and process the raw data so it can be easily accessed and used by people in the business. Most often businesses use computer systems including software for data analysis and hard drives, disks, or tapes to store the data. However, very simple systems may involve file cabinets, a filing system, and data processing procedures.

Input refers to the ways in which information is entered into the information management system. Common methods are computer keyboards, scanners, or transferring files from one computer to another. Information also can be entered by voice in some systems. *Output* refers to the ways in which information is retrieved from the information management system so it can be reviewed and used by managers. Information can be sent to a printer, exchanged via telephone or wireless communication tools, saved as an information file on a diskette, or accessed through the Internet.

Management information is the organized information and reports reviewed by managers and others to aid decision making. The format of information and reports can include text, tables, charts, graphs, pictures, and drawings. Information also can be provided in video and audio formats. Management information is carefully prepared so that it is well-organized, objective, and easy to use.

DEVELOP MANAGEMENT INFORMATION SYSTEMS

People in business today are often called knowledge workers. **Knowledge workers** are people whose jobs require them to regularly access and use information. Managers and non-managers are knowledge workers. An information management system is an important tool for knowledge workers. An effective information management system allows managers and employees to access and share information. Knowledge workers need to input and retrieve information. They have to understand the information and use it to do their work. An important part of using an information management system is to make sure everyone is trained to use the technology and the information.

Information Management Departments Most businesses have a department staffed by specialists who are responsible for maintaining information systems. Those include computer operators, programmers, data entry and clerical personnel, and information system managers. The department is responsible for making sure the necessary information is obtained and stored and that it is easy for people to obtain the information they need.

Global Access Today, with global operations, companies need to be able to obtain and send information at a moment's notice all over the world. Employees will want to be able to access information from a hotel room, airport, or customer's office using a laptop computer, personal digital assistant, or cell phone. Twenty-four hour access through a variety of communication tools is a requirement for many information management systems.

Security An important issue for information management departments is security. Many people need access to information, but they should not be able to see all the information in a business. Much information is private or could be harmful to the business if competitors are able to obtain it. The news media regularly reports on businesses that have had their computer systems attacked by hackers who are able to enter the company's computers and steal, alter, or destroy information. Companies use many strategies to protect information. These strategies include requiring user passwords to access data, saving information as backup files, and scrambling information to make it unreadable to others.

Companies develop firewalls to protect information from outsiders. A *firewall* is special software that screens people who enter and/or exit a computer network. It requests them to enter specific information and then checks the hardware and software being used to gain access. Other methods, including voice verification and retina scanning, are being developed.

Business information needs to be protected from fire, storms, earthquakes, and other disasters. Businesses may maintain backup records at a separate location, often in another city, so the information system can continue to operate in the event of a disaster. They may have backup computer systems and power supplies so equipment failure will not harm the business.

CHECKPOINT

What are the five components of an information management system?

_____

_____

THINK CRITICALLY

1. What are some examples of communication technology that do not use a computer?

_____

_____

_____

2. What are several reasons why a business may choose not to purchase and use a new type of technology?

_____

_____

_____

3. Why should people other than managers have access to information management systems?

_____

_____

_____

4. In what ways can an information management system improve communication in a business?

_____

_____

_____

MAKE CONNECTIONS

5. HISTORY Using information obtained from the Internet, prepare a timeline from 1940 to the present. Identify at least 10 important historical events in the development of computers and the Internet that occurred during that time. Prepare a chart that illustrates the timeline with the events listed in the year each occurred. Record your ideas for the timeline on the lines below.

_____

_____

_____

_____

_____

6. HEALTH One concern in business today is the affect of technology on the health of employees. Examples include wrist injuries from typing on a computer keyboard at the wrong height and the possibility of cancer risks from using cell phones. Using a computer and word-processing software, write a two-page report identifying several health issues related to the use of technology. Report on ways that managers can try to protect the health of employees.

REVIEW

CHAPTER SUMMARY

LESSON 3.1 Business Communication

A. Communication occurs when a sender and receiver have a common understanding of information exchanged.

B. Managers need effective communications skills and should carefully plan the communications they use.

LESSON 3.2 Written and Oral Communication

A. The two common forms of business communication are written and oral communication.

B. Effective writing requires an understanding of grammar, sentence and paragraph structure, and spelling. Effective speaking results from careful preparation, practice, and confidence.

LESSON 3.3 Information Technology

A. The effective use of technology has allowed workers to become more productive and businesses, more efficient.

B. An effective information management system allows managers and employees to access and share information as they work.

VOCABULARY BUILDER

Choose the term that best fits the definition. Write the letter of the answer in the space provided. Some terms may not be used.

_____ **1.** One or more people with whom the sender wants to communicate

_____ **2.** Uses text and images to convey information

_____ **3.** A comprehensive process for obtaining, organizing, storing, and providing information to improve decision-making

_____ **4.** The exchange of information between two or more people in a way that results in common understanding

_____ **5.** The practical application of science and engineering

_____ **6.** The person or organization providing the information

_____ **7.** The use of spoken words, body language, and listening to convey information

_____ **8.** The methods used to move information between senders and receivers

_____ **9.** People whose jobs require them to regularly access and use information

_____ **10.** Involve small numbers of people who come together to address specific business issues

a. communication

b. information managment system

c. knowledge workers

d. media

e. meetings

f. oral communication

g. receiver

h. sender

i. technology

j. written communication

MAKE CONNECTIONS

22. ADVERTISING Collect three print advertisements from magazines and newspapers. Study each ad to see what you believe it is trying to communicate to customers. Using a computer and word processing software, write a paragraph for each advertisement identifying why you believe it is effective or ineffective as a communication tool.

_____

_____

_____

23. SCIENCE Technology is the practical application of science and engineering to improve business operations and procedures. Make a spreadsheet that shows several examples of technology used in business and how operations or procedures are improved as a result of the technology.

_____

_____

_____

24. LANGUAGE Computers and the Internet have introduced many new words into the English language. Examples given in the lesson include _snail mail_ and _firewall._ Talk with people who use computers and the Internet frequently and ask them to identify words or phrases they are familiar with that have specific meaning related to computer and Internet technology. Make a list of the words and their meanings and share them with other class members. See how many terms most students recognize and understand.

_____

_____

25. CAREERS Identify one career in information management, communications, or technology that did not exist ten years ago. Gather information and prepare an oral report that describes the work completed by people in that career, the education and experience requirements, and the technology skills required. Give your report to your class using visual aids.

_____

_____

_____

_____

_____

CHAPTER 4

PRODUCTION, MANUFACTURING, AND MARKETING

LESSONS

CAREERS IN BUSINESS

KINKO'S

In 1970, Paul Orfalea recognized that college students needed to make low-cost photocopies. He opened a small shop next to the University of California at Santa Barbara. Paul named it Kinko's, his nickname because of his curly red hair. Thirty years later Kinko's operates nearly 1,000 stores in nine countries. Kinkos.com makes document production, printing, distribution and other business services available over the Internet. Services have expanded to include videoconferencing, mail and fax services, a computer center, sale of paper and office supplies, and complete document design and production.

If you have a high school diploma, you can be a Project Supervisor at Kinko's. You will be responsible for coworkers, deal with customer service issues, and make sure each project is completed on time and meets quality standards. You will need computer skills, good writing and proofreading skills, and experience in printing or production. Communication, customer-service skills, and being a team player are important.

THINK CRITICALLY

1. Why has Kinko's been successful in adding a variety of products and services?
2. Why must a Project Supervisor have good writing and proofreading skills?

The Chapter 4 video for this module introduces the concepts in this chapter.

PROJECT

Produce and Market a Product

PROJECT OBJECTIVES

■ Describe a procedure for manufacturing a product
■ Outline a procedure for new product development
■ Use research to identify a target market
■ Develop a marketing mix that meets customer needs

GETTING STARTED

Read through the Project Process below. Make a list of materials and information you will need. Decide how you will get the needed materials or information.

■ Your class has decided to produce and sell a "survival pac" for exam week. Divide the class into a production and a marketing team for this project.
■ Agree on three to five items to include in the "survival pac" that can be purchased for a total price of less than $4.

PROJECT PROCESS

Part 1 LESSON 4.1 The "survival pac" will consist of a small paper bag with a design on the bag, the items chosen by the class, a personalized card, and some type of closure for the bag. Organize an assembly procedure for the "survival pacs" to prepare them for distribution.

Part 2 LESSON 4.2 Describe a procedure the class can follow to determine whether a "survival pac" will be a successful new product.

Part 3 LESSON 4.3 Use a simple research procedure to identify the target market for the "survival pac." Describe the characteristics of the target market as completely as possible.

Part 4 LESSON 4.4 Based on your research and target market description, describe all four of the marketing mix elements for the "survival pac."

CHAPTER REVIEW

Project Wrap-up As a class, discuss the decisions made and whether or not those decisions reflect a marketing orientation. Develop several criteria to determine if production and marketing decisions resulted in a successful product.

LESSON 4.1
MANUFACTURING AND SERVICE BUSINESSES

DESCRIBE several ways products are manufactured

IDENTIFY important differences between services and products

PRODUCTION AND MANUFACTURING

Walk down the streets of a shopping area or through a shopping mall in your town or city. Consider the hundreds and thousands of products that are available for sale. Multiply those by the millions of people all over the world who purchase products and services each day.

The U.S. economy and the economies of other countries are based on production and consumption. Businesses produce and distribute the products consumers want and need. Consumers' purchases provide the money businesses need to pay their expenses and make a profit. **Production** is all of the

ON THE $CENE

Jacob and Marcella Korney are ready to buy their first home. They have looked in several neighborhoods and have seen many different types of houses that vary in size, price, and design features. In one neighborhood, the builder brings pieces of the house in on large trucks and then assembles the pieces onsite. In another, customers can select one of four available models. In a third neighborhood, each buyer works with an architect to design a customized house that will be different from any other in the area. What do you think are the advantages and disadvantages of each type of building procedure for the homebuilder and the homebuyer?

activities involved in creating products for sale. **Manufacturing** is a form of production in which raw and semi-finished materials are processed, assembled, or converted into finished products.

Manufacturing is a complex process. Most products are made of several parts. Manufacturers develop the parts or purchase them from other companies. The parts are stored, assembled, and packaged. They are often stored in large warehouses until sold. Then they must be packaged for shipping directly to the customer or to stores where they will be sold to consumers.

TYPES OF MANUFACTURING

When you think of a manufacturing business, you may have an image of a large factory with a long assembly line. While assembly lines are one way to manufacture products, there are many other ways as well.

Mass Production An assembly process that produces a large number of identical products is called *mass production*. It usually involves an assembly line where employees continuously perform the same task to assemble the product. Complex products sold in very large quantities—such as computers, home appliances, and automobiles—are mass-produced. Mass production enables companies to manufacture products at a low cost and in large quantities while maintaining specific quality standards.

Continuous Processing In a second type of manufacturing, *continuous processing*, raw materials constantly move through specially designed equipment. This processing changes their form to make them more useable for consumption or further manufacturing. Steel mills convert iron ore into steel. Oil refineries change crude oil into a variety of petroleum products. Cereal manufacturers process grain into breakfast cereal.

Repetitive Production In *repetitive production*, a manufacturer does the same thing over and over to produce a product. The activity is usually rather simple and can be completed in a short time but is repeated again and again. Bricklayers use repetitive production to construct walls. People who assemble boxes for packaging repeat the same assembly process for each box.

INTERNATIONAL ORGANIZATION FOR STANDARDIZATION

To assure quality in manufactured products distributed globally, many companies choose to comply with ISO standards. These standards are set by the International Organization for Standardization, based in Europe. ISO 9000 standards, first introduced in 1987, assure quality from product design through manufacturing. The ISO 14000 series assures quality on environmental management. The label "ISO" is not an acronym. It was derived from the Greek word "isos," meaning "equal."

THINK CRITICALLY Why do you think some companies choose to undergo the costly and difficult process of achieving ISO certification?

Intermittent Processing Processing that uses short production runs to make predetermined quantities of different products is called *intermittent processing*. An example of a business using intermittent manufacturing is a coffee manufacturer. The company will store a variety of types and grades of coffee beans. When a customer order is received, the correct beans will be selected, roasted, ground, and packaged to fill the order. Then a different blend will be produced for the next customer.

Custom Manufacturing Often there is a need to build only one or a very limited number of units of a product. *Custom manufacturing* is the process used to design and build a unique product to meet the specific needs of the purchaser. Designing a building and writing the code for computer programs are examples of custom manufacturing. A custom manufacturer works closely with a customer to develop a unique product. The company must be flexible enough to design and build a different product each time.

IMPROVE MANUFACTURING

Global competition has put pressure on manufacturers to improve quality and efficiency. **Quality management** is a process for assuring product quality by developing standards for all operations and products and measuring results against those standards. For quality management to succeed, a company must accept no defects and hold all employees responsible for quality.

Technology has contributed to the improvement of manufacturing. Computers have improved the quality and speed of production and reduced costs. Robots now complete many routine and repetitive activities in manufacturing. They also complete much of the dangerous work or tasks requiring precise operations. Computers can check the quality of each product so problems can be corrected. Production schedules can be improved to make sure materials are available when needed and in the correct quantity.

CHECKPOINT

Name five types of manufacturing.

_____

_____

SERVICE BUSINESSES

Service businesses are the fastest growing type of business in the U.S. economy. Consumers spend more than half their money on the purchase of services. Nearly two-thirds of all employees work in service jobs. Service businesses may be large or small companies.

Services are activities of value that do not result in the ownership of anything tangible. There are traditional service businesses such as travel agents, insurance companies, and cleaning services. New products often require service businesses to support them. Today many companies provide services related to the use of computers and the Internet. These include security businesses, web-design companies, and Internet service providers (ISPs).

UNIQUE CHARACTERISTICS OF SERVICES

Services have important characteristics that make them different from products. These differences in form, availability, quality, and timing result in unique operating procedures for service businesses.

Form Services are intangible. That means they do not include a physical product and don't exist once they are consumed. Consider how attending a concert or visiting an aquarium differs from purchasing a CD or owning a tank of fish.

Availability The service cannot be separated from the person or business supplying it. An office building cannot be cleaned without the people who operate the cleaning equipment. A tax service will be unable to complete the yearly tax forms of its customers without an accountant or a tax specialist.

Quality The quality of a service is affected by the people who provide it. When and where the service is provided also affect its quality. A company providing landscaping services needs employees who can operate the equipment and who understand how to maintain healthy lawns, shrubs, and trees.

Timing A service cannot be stored or held until needed. If you arrive at an athletic event after it begins, you will no longer be able to see the entire game. If a bus or train is only half full, it must still follow its scheduled route.

OPERATE A SERVICE BUSINESS

In order to operate a successful service business, the manager must understand the needs of customers and the unique characteristics of services. The needs of customers should determine the type of service to provide as well as when and where to provide it. Because a service is intangible, service providers must find ways to help customers understand what they will receive. Service providers must use effective communication and may provide written information to help the consumer understand and use the service effectively.

The service must be performed in an acceptable way to the customer. A member of a fitness center may want the services of a specific trainer. A banking customer may prefer to use an ATM rather than wait for a teller.

The people providing the service must be well trained. They must understand that the way they serve the customer will affect whether the customer is satisfied or not. An uncaring attitude or poor quality work will result in a dissatisfied customer who may not return to the business.

The quantity of a service provided by the business needs to match the quantity demanded by customers. When a popular movie is released, a theatre may need to schedule it more frequently or show it on several screens.

CHECKPOINT

In what ways do services differ from products?

_____

_____

THINK CRITICALLY

1. What is the relationship between production and consumption?

2. Why are many manufacturers moving away from mass production even though it is more efficient?

3. What are some examples of well-paying service occupations that require a high level of skill or education?

4. Why is careful scheduling of employees important for service businesses?

MAKE CONNECTIONS

5. PROBLEM SOLVING Nancy Framey started a new business where she will complete Internet searches for people who need answers to questions or want information on a specific topic. She is having difficulty explaining the service to prospective customers. Using word-processing software, prepare a brochure Nancy can use to help customers understand the service.

6. THE ARTS Service businesses are a good choice for people who have special talents or have studied the arts. Develop a list of possible service businesses that could be started by a person with talent and preparation in art, music, dance, or acting. Choose one of these service business ideas and present this idea to the class.

LESSON 4.2
NEW PRODUCTS

GOALS

IDENTIFY sources of
new product ideas

OUTLINE a process
for developing new
products

THE IMPORTANCE OF NEW PRODUCTS

Walk down the aisle of any store and look around. A large percentage of
the products you see did not exist even five years ago. Customer needs
change, competitors regularly introduce new products, and improvements are
made to existing products. A business that is not willing or able to improve
its products or develop completely new products will not continue to be
successful. Before a business can offer new products to consumers, it must
complete three steps. If any one of the steps cannot be completed successfully, the product will fail. The company must

1. Develop an idea for a new product that consumers want to buy

2. Turn the idea into a workable product design

3. Produce the product and make it available to consumers at a price they are
   willing to pay

ON THE $CENE

Shantee Loerado is the manager of a company that produces children's
toys. It seems that each year one or two new toys introduced by its
competitors becomes immediately successful. While her company has a
number of good products, it never has had one of the top toys. Shantee
would like to help her company come up with one of those successful new
ideas. Consider new toys that have been successful in the past several years.
Can you help Shantee identify types of toys or sources of ideas for toys that
are likely to be successful?

Choose a product that you use often. Write a questionnaire to be used by the leader of a consumer panel that will find out consumer attitudes and offer suggestions about the product. Share your questionnaire in class.

DEVELOP NEW PRODUCT IDEAS

Less than ten percent of all new product ideas result in a product that is sold to consumers. Few get beyond the idea stage. For those that are produced and offered for sale, more than half will not survive in the market for five years. A business risks a large amount of money in equipment, materials, and personnel to produce a new product. If the product is not successful, that money will be lost. Companies work hard to identify successful new products. Therefore, businesses must identify a process for generating new product ideas. Ideas for new products can come from many sources.

Company Personnel Employees may suggest new product ideas. A company may get ideas from salespeople and production personnel who work with specific products every day. Companies may ask employees to identify new product ideas or improvements for existing products. The employees may receive money or other types of recognition for ideas that lead to profitable products. Many companies employ people whose primary responsibility is to create and test new products.

Customers Current customers are a very good source of product ideas. Based on their experience with the company's products and the products of competitors, they know what they like and don't like. They will be able to identify ideas for improvements and for new products. Companies obtain information from customers by sending them surveys, calling them to ask questions, or asking customers to call or e-mail the company with suggestions and ideas. Salespeople also may gather information from customers by talking with them and listening carefully to questions and concerns.

Consumers People who are not current customers also are a good source of information. Consumer research gathers information about the experience and opinions of prospective customers. A company can form a *consumer panel*—a group of people who offer opinions about the company's products and services. The panel meets frequently to discuss the members' opinions about new products. It may also offer suggestions on ways the company can improve its current products.

Companies often conduct research in places where consumers shop, such as a mall or large store. The research may involve asking customers a short series of questions about their experiences with products. Or, it may involve a

more complicated process in which consumers are shown samples of new products and asked detailed questions about them. The Internet is now being used to survey consumers about product preferences.

Product Research Product research is research completed by engineers and other scientists to develop new products or to discover improvements for existing products. Researchers conduct experiments and tests without a specific product in mind in order to make discoveries that might lead to new products. They also can study existing products to solve problems or identify possible design improvements.

Describe several sources a company should consider to develop ideas for new products and improvements to existing products?

_____

_____

did you KNOW?

The highest new product failure rate is for consumer products. The failure rate for new industrial products and new services is much lower. What are some possible reasons for the differences?

DESIGN NEW PRODUCTS

Developing a list of possible new products is just the first step in a complicated new product development procedure. The company must determine which of the ideas can be produced and marketed successfully. Planning and producing a new product involves all of the major departments in a business including production, finance, human resources, and marketing. Usually specific managers in a company have responsibility for directing the process and coordinating the efforts of everyone involved.

DETERMINE FEASIBILITY

A successful new product should be designed to meet customer needs. Customers should be able to identify features of the new product that are different from and better than those of competing products. Also, products need to be safe and easy to use. They must meet all state and federal laws for product quality and environmental and consumer safety. You can probably identify several examples of new products that were introduced and then had to be recalled because of safety issues or other problems.

DESIGN A MODEL

If the company has a new product idea that has a good chance for consumer acceptance and meets safety and legal standards, the company will begin to design the product. In this step, engineers and researchers build models of the product and test them to be sure that the company can design a quality product. The design process checks factors such as durability, ease of use, and a pleasing appearance. Before the company makes the large investment needed to produce the model, it usually performs a great deal of testing to be sure it meets all requirements for success. When a model is available, the company can use it for additional consumer research.

IDENTIFY RESOURCES

Once a model has been built and tested, the company must determine all of the resources it will need to produce large quantities of the product. It may have to buy production facilities and equipment or modify those it currently uses to produce other products. If the company plans to use existing facilities and equipment, it will need a production schedule that shows how it can

WORKSHOP

As a class, make a list of products that are no longer sold or have undergone major changes. Review the list and determine why you think the original product is no longer successful.

produce the new products without disrupting the production of current products. Employees who have the skills to produce and sell the new product will be needed. The company may need to hire new employees or shift current employees to the production of the new product.

DETERMINE PROFITABILITY

After all planning has been completed, the company will determine the costs of producing the product and compare those costs to the price it will charge for the product. This requires a careful study of competing products and consumer preferences to set a fair price. It is possible that customers are not willing to pay a price that will cover all of the research, design, production and marketing costs. In this case, the company will decide not to produce the product. If the company can make the decision to halt development at this point, it will incur less financial loss than if it produces a large quantity that goes unsold or must be sold at a loss.

MANAGE NEW PRODUCT DEVELOPMENT

The process for developing a successful new product is complex and time consuming. It involves gathering and reviewing information from many sources inside and outside the company. The efforts of many people need to be coordinated. Risky decisions have to be made that can result in new customers and higher profits, or dissatisfied customers and losses for the company.

An important position in many companies is the product or brand manager. People who hold that position are responsible for managing all of the

activities described above as well as managing the products after they have been introduced to the market. Product and brand managers must be able to gather and study a great deal of information, work effectively with many people, and make very difficult decisions. People responsible for new products need to have a great deal of business experience. They must be able to understand research and financial information. Finally, they must be willing to take responsibility for the results of their decisions about the new product.

CHECKPOINT

What steps should a company follow to successfully plan a new product?

_____

_____

THINK CRITICALLY

1. Why do most new product ideas never result in a product that is successfully sold to consumers?

_____
_____
_____
_____

2. When developing new product ideas, what benefits result from gathering information from both consumers who are and are not current customers of a business?

_____
_____
_____

3. Do you think successful new product ideas can be developed without doing any consumer research? Why or why not?

_____
_____
_____
_____

4. How can a company determine the price consumers are willing to pay for a product before the new product is actually produced?

_____
_____
_____

MAKE CONNECTIONS

5. SCIENCE Use a science textbook, an encyclopedia, or the Internet to identify and list the steps in scientific decision making. Describe how engineers or researchers in a company should use the scientific decision-making steps to conduct new product research.

_____
_____
_____
_____
_____

6. TECHNOLOGY Join with several other students and develop a five-question survey to identify which brands of personal computers and which features of computers consumers prefer. Have at least ten people complete the survey. Provide your findings in a spreadsheet format. The report should include both tables and graphs.

LESSON 4.3
MARKETING BASICS

DESCRIBE the marketing concept and the parts of a marketing strategy

IDENTIFY two important tools used to make marketing decisions

EFFECTIVE MARKETING

When some people hear the term *marketing* they think only of advertising and selling. However, marketing is much more than that. Marketing is an important business function that connects the business with its customers. Marketing is used to identify the needs of customers, help the business develop the products and services that meet customer needs, and make the products and services available to customers when and where they want them. Without effective marketing, customer needs would not be satisfied and the business would not be profitable.

Marketing is creating, distributing, pricing, and promoting products and services to meet customer needs at a profit. Marketing is an important economic activity because it connects production and consumption. Marketers use the *marketing concept* to plan a *marketing strategy*.

ON THE $CENE

Jai Huan planned to purchase a new portable CD player to replace his old one that no longer worked well. By talking with his friends and looking in stores he knew that he could choose from many brands, each of which offered a number of features. It appeared he could pay as little as $25 or as much as $200. He wanted a durable player that would take the bumps and knocks of regular use. It should have good sound quality and be easy to use. He also expected it to last for several years, especially if he chose one of the more expensive models. How would you advise Jai to gather information and compare models in order to make the best choice?

THE MARKETING CONCEPT

Many years ago, companies didn't think much about marketing. They produced products that they thought consumers would buy and made sure the products were distributed to places where customers could buy them. If the products did not sell as well as expected, the company might increase advertising or reduce the price to encourage consumers to buy.

Today, customers have more and more choices of products and services to buy. They also have access to a great deal of information so they can make better purchasing decisions. Successful companies now use the marketing concept. The **marketing concept** keeps the needs of the consumer uppermost in mind during the design, production, and distribution of a product. Companies using the marketing concept focus on consumer needs. They are customer-oriented in that they direct the activities of the company at satisfying customers. When customers are satisfied they will continue to purchase the products and services of a company and it will be able to make a profit.

MARKETING STRATEGY

A company's **marketing strategy** is all of the important decisions made to successfully market a product or service. A marketing strategy is made up of two elements: the *target market* and the *marketing mix*. The marketing strategy answers two questions.

1. To whom will we sell our product or service?

2. What will we offer our customers to satisfy their needs?

Most companies offer many products and services for sale. A unique marketing strategy may be required for different products and services.

Target Market A group of customers that has very similar needs, and to whom the company plans to sell its product, is called a **target market**. A company can more easily produce a product that will satisfy everyone in the target market. If people have needs that are quite different, it will be almost impossible to develop a product that will satisfy each of them. Imagine planning a product like a chair. It can be made in a variety of designs and shapes with a number of special features. No one chair design will satisfy everyone's needs. People sitting all day in an office will want something quite different from those buying a chair to watch television. It would be impossible to design one or even a few chairs to meet all possible needs. If you can identify a group of

MARKETING VIA THE INTERNET The Internet has become a very important marketing tool. Many companies have web sites on which they advertise their products and services. Customers also may place orders using the Internet. Then they can track delivery of purchased items by checking the web sites of FedEx, UPS, or the U.S. Postal Service. Marketing services on the Web are expected to expand dramatically every year.

THINK CRITICALLY What are some other examples of Internet marketing?

people with similar needs, you could successfully design chairs that meet the needs of that group. A company may identify several target markets. Each target market will require something different to satisfy its needs.

Marketing Mix Marketing is made up of four elements known as the *four Ps of marketing*. The four Ps are *product, price, place,* and *promotion*. The blending of all decisions related to the four elements of marketing is called the **marketing mix**. The marketing mix for a new product may be to design the item for young working professionals, give it a high price, sell it using an Internet web site, and advertise it in business magazines. Or it could be to produce a mid-priced item to be advertised on television and sold through specialty retail stores to the parents of children. Can you identify a possible marketing mix for the CD player Jai Huan wants to buy?

CHECKPOINT ✓

What are the two decisions that make up a marketing strategy?

_____

_____

MARKETING PLANNING TOOLS

Marketing decisions must be made carefully if the results will satisfy customers' needs while allowing the company to make a profit. Two tools are used by marketing managers to develop effective marketing mixes—*the product life cycle* and *consumer product categories*.

THE PRODUCT LIFE CYCLE

Successful products move through rather predictable stages throughout their product lives. They are introduced, and then their sales and profits increase rapidly until they reach a point at which they level off. Eventually, both profits and sales will decline, as newer products replace the old ones. The *product life cycle* is the four stages of sales and profit performance through which all products progress. The four stages are *introduction, growth, maturity,* and *decline*. The figure illustrates how sales and profits change at the different stages of the product life cycle.

WORKSHOP

As a class, agree on three products to analyze. Then individually select the stage of the product life cycle and consumer product category you think is the best fit for each product. Compare and discuss your decisions in class.

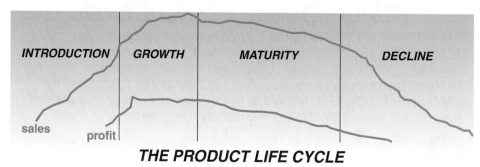

INTRODUCTION   GROWTH   MATURITY   DECLINE

sales

profit

THE PRODUCT LIFE CYCLE

Introduction Stage In the *introduction stage*, a brand-new product enters the market. The new product is quite different from and better than the products customers are currently using. The costs of producing and marketing a new product are usually high, and at first result in a loss or low profits. The company counts on future sales to make a profit. If a product is introduced successfully, more and more consumers will buy it and sales will start to grow rapidly.

Growth Stage When competitors see the success of the new product, they will want to get into that market as well. When several brands of the new product are available and sales begin to increase rapidly, the market moves into the *growth stage*. Most companies make a profit in this stage.

Maturity Stage A product in the *maturity stage* has been purchased by many customers and has become quite profitable. The product has many competing brands with very similar features. Customers have a hard time identifying differences among brands but may have developed a loyalty to one or a very few brands. In this stage, companies spend a lot on promotion and reduce prices. Profits usually fall even though sales may still increase.

Decline Stage Many products stay in the maturity stage for a long time. However, sooner or later products move into a decline stage. The *decline stage* occurs when a new product is introduced that is much better or easier to use, and customers begin to switch from the old product to the new product. As more and more customers are attracted to the new product, the companies selling the old product will soon see declines in both profits and sales.

CONSUMER PRODUCT CATEGORIES

Marketers group products into three categories—convenience goods, shopping goods, and specialty goods.

Convenience Goods Inexpensive items that consumers purchase regularly without a great deal of thought are *convenience goods*. Consumers are not willing to shop around for these products because they purchase them often, the many competing products do not differ much from each other, and they don't cost much. Examples are candy, milk, and soft drinks.

Shopping Goods Products that consumers purchase less frequently than convenience goods, usually have a higher price, and require some buying thought are *shopping goods*. Customers see important differences between brands of these products in terms of price and features. Therefore, they are willing to shop at several businesses and compare products and brands before they make a purchase. Cars, large appliances, and houses are examples.

Specialty goods Products that customers insist upon having and are willing to search for until they find them are *specialty goods*. Customers who decide that only one product or brand will satisfy them will shop until they locate and buy that brand. Examples are designer clothing and fine jewelry.

CHECKPOINT

Name the four stages of the product life cycle.

_____

_____

THINK CRITICALLY

1. Why do many people think only of selling and advertising when they hear the term *marketing*?

_____

_____

_____

_____

_____

2. Why should companies identify target markets before developing a marketing mix?

_____

_____

_____

_____

3. How would a product in the maturity stage of the life cycle be marketed differently from one in the introduction stage?

_____

_____

_____

_____

MAKE CONNECTIONS

4. PSYCHOLOGY Marketers plan marketing strategies to respond to consumers' needs. Abraham Maslow developed a theory that described five levels of needs. Gather information on Maslow's hierarchy of needs and develop a graphic that illustrates the five levels of need. Present the graphic you developed to your class. Then discuss each level with other students in your class to determine how a business could use that information to effectively market a product.

_____

_____

_____

_____

5. MARKETING You are a consultant for a bicycle manufacturer. Identify two unique target markets that the manufacturer might consider serving. Make sure to provide a description of the people you think are in the target market and the unique needs of each market. Then identify the type of bicycle that you think would best meet the needs of each target market. Organize your findings in a spreadsheet.

LESSON 4.4
MARKETING MIX

GOALS

DESCRIBE the importance of product and place decisions

DISCUSS how businesses plan pricing and promotion

PRODUCT AND PLACE

Recall the marketing mix elements—product, place, price, and promotion. Each element must be planned carefully to respond to important customer needs in ways that are better than the choices offered by competitors.

Product A *product* is all attributes, both tangible and intangible, that customers receive in exchange for the purchase price. It includes both physical goods and services. Some products are very simple and easy for the customer to understand and use, while others are very complex. Businesspeople and consumers usually hold very different perceptions of a product. Businesspeople think of their products as what they have to offer to customers.

ON THE $CENE

Jordan McHue is a veteran retailer. Over his 40-year career, he has managed and owned retail businesses in many different product areas. Jordan knows that competition in retailing moves through a rather predictable cycle known as the wheel of retailing. A new type of business will often start with a limited choice of products, few services, and low prices. As more businesses begin to compete, they will offer greater choices of products, more services, expanded facilities, and higher prices. Ask people who remember the first fast-food restaurants to describe the menu, prices, and locations of those businesses. What other examples of the wheel of retailing can you identify? Why do you think competition always seems to follow the same cycle?

Place Once a product has been produced, the business needs to get the product to the customer. That marketing process is known as *distribution*. Place as a marketing mix element includes decisions about how and when products will be distributed and who is responsible for distribution. No matter how good a product is, it will not be sold unless the company fills orders correctly and delivers the products undamaged and on time to the correct locations.

EFFECTIVE PRODUCT PLANNING

Because of the variety of customer needs, the uses for products, and the number of competing companies producing and selling products, product

development decisions must be made carefully. Companies must produce the right products in the right quantities with the features and services customers need. If they don't, they will quickly lose out to competitors who make better product decisions.

Product Features A company begins with a *basic product* which is a very simple design that meets important needs of a target market. To meet more specific needs and to increase the usefulness of the product, the company adds *product features*. For example, an electric alarm clock may have a battery backup or a lighted dial that can be seen in the dark. A snooze feature allows you to get an extra ten minutes of sleep in the morning while being assured that the alarm will wake you up again.

Brand Name A company tries to build customer loyalty for its products. That means that when customers purchase a product and like it, the company wants them to be able to buy the same product again. That can be done with the use of brand names. A *brand* is a name, symbol, word, or design that identifies a product, service, or company. Brands are important to consumers because they want to be comfortable with the purchases they make. Have you shopped in a store that offers generic products that do not have a brand name? What are your feelings when you seen them?

Packaging An important part of product development is packaging. A package provides protection while the product is being shipped and stored. The individual container for the product also prevents damage during use by the consumer and may even offer security to keep the product from being lost or stolen. Packaging provides important product information to customers such as product composition, special features, and proper use.

DISTRIBUTE PRODUCTS TO CONSUMERS

The routes products follow while moving from the producer to the consumer, including all related activities and participating organizations, are called *channels of distribution*. When producers sell directly to the ultimate consumer, it is called *direct distribution*. When distribution takes place through other businesses, it is called *indirect distribution*.

Determining the number and type of businesses and the activities they will perform in a channel of distribution is an important decision. Adding businesses to the channel makes the channel more complex and difficult to control. However, using businesses that have particular expertise in transportation, product handling, or other distribution activities may result in improved distribution or actual cost savings.

Companies use telemarketing as the primary form of direct marketing. More than 10 million people sell products, process orders, or package and ship products customers purchase by telephone.

Lost, late, or damaged products are of little value to customers. Transportation methods and product handling are important parts of the distribution process. Another important factor in effective product distribution is taking and processing orders so customers get the correct products in the quantities they need. Orders can be taken in person, by telephone or mail order, or using the Internet. Finally, customers expect effective customer service to be able to get answers to questions, help in using the product, and assistance with problems.

CHECKPOINT

What are the important marketing decisions involved in distributing products to meet customer needs?

_____

_____

PLAN PRICE AND PROMOTION

The final two elements of the marketing mix are price and promotion. *Price* is the amount of money given to acquire a product. The product must be priced so buyers consider it a good value and so the business is able to make a profit. *Promotion* is providing information to consumers that will assist them in making a decision and persuade them to purchase a product or service. While businesses have many choices of ways to promote their products and services, the major methods are advertising and personal selling.

BUSINESS MATH CONNECTION

Determine the margin and net profit for a product that sells for $5.00 per unit, has cost of goods sold of $2.20 per unit, and operating expenses of $2.35 per unit.

SOLUTION

Managers use the following formulas to determine the margin and net profit.

Selling Price − Cost of Goods Sold = Margin
$5.00 − $2.20 = $2.80

Margin − Operating expenses = Net profit
$2.80 − $2.35 = $0.45

The margin is $2.80 and the net profit is $0.45.

Using all four Ps, describe two different marketing mixes for cell phone service. Compare your decisions with those of other class members. Discuss how a business could decide which marketing mix to use from the many possible choices.

SET THE PRICE

Prices must be carefully planned to achieve both objectives of satisfying customers and making a product. There are several parts of a product's price. The *selling price* is the actual price customers pay for the product. The largest cost that the price must cover is the *cost of goods sold.* That is the cost to the business of producing the product or buying it for resale. The selling price must also cover operating expenses. *Operating expenses* are the costs of operating a business. The *margin* is the difference between the selling price and the cost of goods sold. Finally, *net profit* is the difference between the selling price and all costs and expenses of the business.

Businesses usually have a choice of prices they can charge and still make a profit. Some businesses price their products very high but offer a high level of customer service. They usually will sell fewer products but make a higher net profit on each product sold. Other businesses will try to price as low as possible. Even though they will make little profit per item, they expect to sell a higher volume of products. A third choice may be to set prices close to the competitors' prices. This prevents the competition from attracting customers by offering lower prices. This type of pricing usually is necessary when customers have many choices and do not prefer a particular brand.

METHODS OF PROMOTION

Many good products and services go unsold because customers are not aware of them or how they can satisfy customer needs. Promotion is the primary way that businesses communicate with prospective customers. Businesses use promotion to inform consumers about the features and benefits of their products and services and to encourage them to buy.

Advertising is any form of paid promotion that delivers a message to many people at the same time. Because the message is designed to appeal to many people, it will be rather impersonal. However, because the message will reach thousands of people, the cost of communicating with each person is very low. Common types of advertising are television, newspaper, magazine, and radio. The Internet is growing in importance as a way for businesses to advertise.

Personal selling is promotion through direct, personal contact with a customer. The salesperson usually makes direct contact with the customer through a face-to-face meeting. Salespeople are able to learn about the specific needs of customers and match the correct product and services to that need. Selling complex or technical products is a difficult task and requires a great deal of skill. Often teams of salespeople meet several times with a number of people to make a sale. Because of the importance of selling to businesses, salespeople often are among the highest paid people in a company.

What is the purpose of promotion?

_____

_____

THINK CRITICALLY

1. How does the decision made about one marketing mix element affect the other mix elements?

_____

_____

_____

_____

2. Why is it possible for one business to charge higher prices for the same products than a competing business?

_____

_____

_____

_____

_____

3. What are some things that make an advertisement memorable? Is a memorable advertisement always effective? Why or why not?

_____

_____

_____

_____

MAKE CONNECTIONS

4. BUSINESS MATH Make the calculations to fill in the blanks in the table.

Selling Price	Cost of Goods Sold	Margin	Operating Expenses	Net Profit
$1.00	$0.40		$ 0.45	
	$3.20	$4.00		$1.20
$15.50		$7.60		$3.85

5. TECHNOLOGY Search the Internet to identify several types of advertising. Either print copies of each advertisement or create a drawing of the advertisement. For each advertisement describe the target market and the marketing mix being used by the company.

_____

_____

_____

6. DEBATE Divide the class into teams to debate the following issue. Does advertising help people make more informed purchasing decisions, or does it cause people to purchase products or services they do not need?

CHAPTER SUMMARY

LESSON 4.1 Manufacturing and Service Businesses

A. Products are manufactured in many ways ranging from mass production to custom manufacturing.

B. Managers must understand needs of customers and the unique characteristics of services.

LESSON 4.2 New Products

A. To offer new products to consumers, a business must develop an idea, turn the idea into a workable product design, and produce the product.

B. Developing a successful new product is a complex process.

LESSON 4.3 Marketing Basics

A. Without effective marketing, customer needs would not be satisfied and the business would not be profitable.

B. A marketing strategy is made up of the target market and marketing mix.

LESSON 4.4 Marketing Mix

A. Consumers have many choices for almost any product or service they want to purchase.

B. The marketing mix includes all of the marketing resources a business can control in order to satisfy customer needs at a profit.

VOCABULARY BUILDER

Choose the term that best fits the definition. Write the letter of the answer in the space provided. Some terms may not be used.

_____ **1.** Developing standards for all operations and products and measuring results against those standards

_____ **2.** Completed by engineers and other scientists to develop new products or to discover improvements for existing products

_____ **3.** All of the important decisions made to successfully market a product or service

_____ **4.** All of the activities involved in creating products for sale

_____ **5.** Creating, distributing, pricing, and promoting products and services to meet customer needs at a profit

_____ **6.** Activities of value that do not result in the ownership of anything tangible

_____ **7.** Keeping the needs of the consumer uppermost in mind during the design, production, and distribution of a product

_____ **8.** A form of production in which raw and semi-finished materials are processed, assembled, or converted into finished products

_____ **9.** Gathers information about the experience and opinions of prospective customers

a. consumer research

b. manufacturing

c. marketing

d. marketing concept

e. marketing mix

f. marketing strategy

g. product research

h. production

i. quality management

j. services

k. target market

POINT YOUR BROWSER

b2000.swep.com

REVIEW CONCEPTS

10. What are five types of manufacturing used to develop new products for customers?

_____

_____

_____

_____

11. Describe four characteristics that make services different from products.

_____

_____

_____

_____

12. Identify several sources companies can use to develop new product ideas.

_____

_____

_____

_____

13. A business should complete two steps in developing a marketing strategy. What are those steps?

_____

_____

_____

_____

14. Place the four stages of the product life cycle in the correct order from first stage to last stage.

_____

_____

_____

_____

15. What are the four Ps that make up a marketing mix?

_____

_____

_____

_____

APPLY WHAT YOU LEARNED

16. Why are service businesses the fastest growing part of the U.S. economy?

_____

_____

_____

_____

17. Why should businesses gather information from consumers before planning new products?

_____

_____

_____

18. Identify several products that fit into each of the consumer products categories.

_____

_____

_____

_____

19. How can a brand name and packaging be considered a part of promotion as well as a part of the product?

_____

_____

_____

_____

20. How does the use of credit affect the price that is charged for a product by a business and the perception of that price by customers?

_____

_____

_____

_____

21. How can a business decide whether to use television, radio, newspaper, or magazine advertising as a part of its marketing mix for a product or service?

_____

_____

_____

MAKE CONNECTIONS

22. MANUFACTURING Use the Internet or business directory of your telephone book and find examples of businesses that match each of the types of manufacturing described in Lesson 4.1. Provide a reason for each decision.

_____

_____

_____

_____

23. RESEARCH Identify a product or service that you would like to study. Prepare a survey of at least five questions that can be used to determine how the product or service could be improved. Have at least 10 people complete the survey. Using word processing software, summarize the results in a written report that includes both a table and graph.

24. PSYCHOLOGY Advertising is most effective when it is based on an understanding of consumer needs. Select four newspaper or magazine advertisements for review. For each advertisement, identify the target market for the product being advertised. Then identify the most important consumer need you think the advertisement is addressing. Describe what parts of the advertisement were most effective in responding to the need you identified. Present your findings in class.

_____

_____

_____

_____

25. BUSINESS MATH Use the Internet to identify a web site that compares the prices of products. Identify three products that you would like to compare prices. Using the web site, identify the highest and lowest prices at which the each product is offered for sale. For each product, calculate the difference between the high and low price and the percentage of savings if you purchased the lowest price product. Use spreadsheet software to do the calculations and to prepare a chart to illustrate the information.

_____

_____

_____

_____

_____

CAREERS IN BUSINESS

U.S. SMALL BUSINESS ADMINISTRATION

Since 1953, the Small Business Administration (SBA) has provided support to people who start new businesses. Through local offices in every state, the SBA provides free counseling, education, planning tools and materials, and financial assistance.

The SBA manages federal programs that assist women and minority owned businesses to gain government contracts. The SBA also offers programs to help small business owners qualify for loans and other types of financing.

Business Advisors offer counseling and training for new business owners. They also help prepare business plans and develop financial records. To be a Business Advisor, you need several years of experience operating and managing a business. Experienced advisors may not have a college degree, but younger advisors usually have a bachelor's or master's degree in business or a related area.

THINK CRITICALLY
1. Why does the U.S. government want to help small businesses succeed?
2. Do you think business education or business experience is more important for a Business Advisor? Why?

FINANCIAL MANAGEMENT

LESSONS

5.1 FINANCE A BUSINESS

5.2 FINANCIAL SERVICES

5.3 FINANCIAL RECORDS

5.4 CREDIT AND INSURANCE

The Chapter 5 video for this module introduces the concepts in this chapter.

PROJECT

Achieve Financial Success

PROJECT OBJECTIVES

- ◼ Describe how to finance a new business
- ◼ Identify the financial services needed to operate a business
- ◼ Understand why financial records are needed in a business
- ◼ Protect a business with effective credit plans and insurance

GETTING STARTED

Read through the Project Process below. Make a list of any materials you will need. Decide how you will obtain the needed materials or information.
- ◼ Gather information that describes business services offered by banks from the Internet or by contacting a local bank.

PROJECT PROCESS

Part 1 LESSON 1.1 Identify at least three sources of financing available to a new small business and describe the advantages and disadvantages of each.

Part 2 LESSON 1.2 In small groups identify services that banks and other financial institutions offer to businesses. Agree on those most important and least important to the financial success of a new business.

Part 3 LESSON 1.3 Use the Internet to find information on an accounting software package designed for small businesses. Then make a list of the types of financial records that can be maintained using the software.

Part 4 LESSON 1.4 In your groups, write three policies a small business should have when granting credit to customers or using credit to finance business purchases or operations.

CHAPTER REVIEW

Project Wrap-up Discuss in class the mistakes new businesses make that result in financial problems and what owners can do to achieve financial success.

LESSON 5.1
FINANCE A BUSINESS

GOALS

RECOGNIZE the ways businesses are financed

DESCRIBE factors to consider in financing business operations

HOW TO FINANCE A BUSINESS

The financial strength of a business is one of the most important factors in its success. Poor financial management is one of the primary reasons businesses fail. Business owners need to have adequate resources to finance business operations and must be effective financial managers to use those resources effectively. **Capital** refers to the financial resources used to operate a business. There are several sources of capital for a business. Each source has advantages and disadvantages.

A business needs money to purchase or rent buildings, obtain equipment, raw materials, and supplies needed to operate the business, hire employees, and pay for the day-to-day operating expenses. That money comes from one of two sources. Financial resources the owners of a business provide is **equity capital**. Money obtained from sources other than business owners is **debt capital**. Debt capital is obtained when a business borrows money or obtains credit to purchase products or services.

ON THE $CENE

Arturo's computer repair business has been open almost two years and he has done quite well. However, he now needs to invest in new equipment that might cost as much as $50,000. Arturo is not quite sure how to obtain the money. He could find a partner to invest in the business or try to obtain a loan from a bank. The loan would result in high interest payments for several years. Are there other ways Arturo can obtain the needed money? What recommendation would you make to him?

SOURCES OF EQUITY CAPITAL

A business owner's personal resources are a common source of equity capital. An owner might invest personal savings or use the value of a home or other assets to obtain a personal loan. The owner then invests money from the loan in the business. Because the owner rather than the business is responsible for repaying the loan, that money is considered equity capital.

When one person owns a business, the sources of equity capital are limited to the resources of that individual. Often partnerships are formed so that two or more people can share the ownership and more financial resources are available to be invested in the business.

If a business makes a profit, those profits can be removed from the business for the personal use of the owners. If the profits remain in the business and are available to pay for business operations, they are known as *retained earnings*. Retained earnings are another source of equity capital.

Corporations sell stock to raise money for business operations. Stockholders are actually owners of a business. That means there are literally hundreds and thousands of owners of large corporations. The money people invest when they purchase stock is an important source of equity capital.

OBTAIN DEBT CAPITAL

When owners do not have additional money to invest in a business and retained earnings are not adequate, the business will need to borrow money if financing is needed. When a business needs a large amount of money to purchase a building or expensive equipment, it will need long-term financing. *Long-term financing* is a loan for more than a year and often for 10 to 20 years. For smaller amounts, or to obtain money to meet immediate needs, short-term financing is used. *Short-term financing* is a loan for less than a year and often must be repaid in 30 to 90 days.

The most common source of debt financing is a loan from a bank or other financial institution such as a mortgage company. A business that has a good financial record can obtain an *open line of credit*. That is a specific amount of money available to a business whenever financing is needed. The business has approval to write checks for any amount up to the limit established on the line of credit. An open line of credit is most often used for the expenses of normal business operations.

There are several other sources of debt capital. A vendor may grant credit as an incentive to purchase its products. The business may have 30 to 60 days to pay the bill, which is a form of a loan. If a business has a large amount of *accounts receivable*, or money owed to the business by its customers, it may sell those accounts to another company that will then collect the payments. The selling company will receive much less for the accounts than they are worth.

CHECKPOINT ✓

What is the difference between equity capital and debt capital?

_____

_____

SUCCESSFUL FINANCIAL PLANNING

From time to time most business owners face the question, "How do I obtain the financing necessary to successfully operate the business?" The question has to be answered when a new business is opened, when a successful business wants to expand, or when an existing business is facing financial problems due to competition, increasing costs, or poor sales. Each situation will require a different financial solution.

FACTORS AFFECTING FINANCIAL DECISIONS

A business experiencing financial problems will probably have few choices in obtaining financing. Therefore it is better to do financial planning when the business is doing well and people want to invest in the business. The important factors when deciding on financing are ownership, cost of financing, and financing requirements.

Ownership When equity capital is used and the current owners do not provide the additional money, ownership is given to the people who offer the financing. If a partnership is established, the new partner will become a business owner and will participate in running the company. If the company sells stock to raise capital, the stockholders will be new owners of the business and will have the opportunity to vote on issues affecting business activities and operations. The new owners also will share in any new profits.

Debt equity does not offer ownership. The person or company providing a loan or extending credit receives interest on the amount loaned but cannot directly influence decisions about business operations. Once the loan is repaid, those who provided the loan have no future claims on the business.

Cost of Financing Each type of financing has a different cost to a business. When a business receives a bank loan, the loan will have an interest rate. There can be major differences in the interest rates charged. The interest rate will

GLOBAL TRADE EXPANSION

The Export-Import Bank of the United States encourages companies to sell products in other countries, especially developing nations. To increase exports the Bank offers a number of services to U.S. businesses. These include assisting businesses to obtain loans to produce exports, offering insurance to protect companies if international buyers do not pay for purchases, and extending credit to foreign buyers so they can purchase U.S. companies' products and services. An important reason the Export-Import Bank was developed was to create jobs in U.S. businesses.

THINK CRITICALLY How does financial support for exporting affect the number of people employed in the United States?

affect the total amount the business pays for the loan. For example, a bank may charge a customer 9 percent for a one-year loan. If the business owner borrowed the money using a credit card, the interest rate might be 16 percent. If $10,000 is borrowed for one year, an additional $700 must be paid to the credit card company since, at 16 percent, interest is $1600 and, at 9 percent, interest is $900.

Equity financing would appear to have no cost because interest is not paid to the new partner or stockholder for the money they invest. However, the new owners will share in any profits as well as own a part of the business. This means the original owners will have a lower percentage. However, the financing may result in a more valuable business with larger profits.

Financing Requirements Whenever financing is provided for a business, there are requirements that the business must meet. A loan has a specific payment schedule. In addition the borrower usually has to pledge some company property, such as buildings, vehicles, equipment, or inventory, to the lender in case the loan is not repaid. If a vendor offers credit, a company may be required to purchase a certain quantity of merchandise and pay for it within a specific time period, such as 30 days. When offering stock for sale, legal requirements affect the rights of the new stockholders. Any financing requirements should be carefully reviewed to make sure the business will be able to meet them and they do not harm the business or the current owners.

FINANCE A NEW BUSINESS

Many people want to become a business owner and even have the enthusiasm and knowledge needed to operate a business. However, they are unable to achieve their dream because they cannot obtain financing. Banks are reluctant to provide a loan when a business cannot demonstrate profitability. Vendors don't want to risk extending credit to a company that does not yet have any sales. Unless the business is being started by an experienced and successful businessperson or offers an unusually attractive product or service, stockholders will be reluctant to invest in the business.

A new business owner will have to invest a substantial amount of his or her own money in the business. This will require several years of working in another business to save money. New business owners often mortgage their homes to get the necessary money. They may ask family members or friends to invest in the new business.

The Small Business Administration and other state and local government agencies have funds to invest in new businesses that have strong business and financial plans. Those agencies also work with banks to reduce the interest rates charged for loans to the new business. State and local governments may offer reduced tax rates or other financial benefits to encourage new business development.

As a class, identify the sources of financing available to businesses in your community. You may want to use a telephone directory to help with the identification. Discuss the advantages and disadvantages of each source.

CHECKPOINT

What factors should a business owner consider when deciding how to obtain financing for the business?

_____

_____

THINK CRITICALLY

1. Why can a company with good products and services fail due to poor financial management?

_____

_____

_____

2. Other than financing, why would the owner of a business want to offer ownership opportunities to a partner?

_____

_____

_____

3. Why would a company that is making a profit still need to obtain financing?

_____

_____

_____

4. How will a carefully prepared business plan help a business owner obtain financing from a bank?

_____

_____

_____

MAKE CONNECTIONS

5. BUSINESS MATH The total interest paid on a loan is calculated using the following formula:

$$\text{Loan amount} \times \frac{\text{Interest rate}}{100} \times \frac{\text{Number of months}}{12} = \text{Total interest}$$

Use spreadsheet software to determine the total interest for each of the following loans.

$8,000 at 12% for 6 months _____

$50,000 at 9% for 12 months _____

$180,000 at 7% for 2 years _____

6. U.S. GOVERNMENT Using the Internet or library resources, identify several federal agencies that offer financial assistance to business. Write a short statement for each agency describing the type of assistance provided and how a business can qualify for the assistance.

_____

_____

_____

_____

_____

LESSON 5.2
FINANCIAL SERVICES

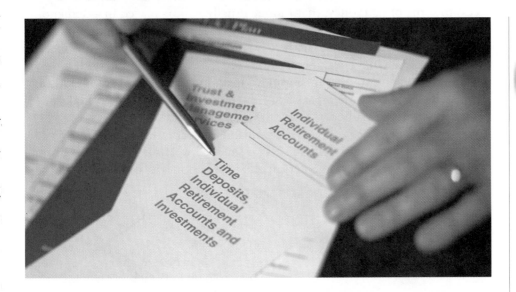

DESCRIBE common financial services needed by businesses

IDENTIFY several financial institutions that serve businesses

FINANCIAL SERVICES FOR BUSINESSES

Money is an important part of most business activities. Businesses need money to purchase land, buildings, and equipment. Employees receive wages and salaries for their work. Businesses that supply products, materials, and supplies used in production and operations must be paid. Customers use cash, checks, and credit cards to purchase products and services. Money is needed to pay taxes, to obtain licenses, and to meet other government regulations. Profits are invested to earn additional money for the business. The owners of small businesses are responsible for financial decisions while larger businesses employ financial managers. However, all businesses use the services of financial institutions. Common types of financial services are managing deposits and savings, providing loans, and offering investment choices.

ON THE $CENE

Philip Gainey knew his recording business could not be successful without the support he received from Capital Bank. He first used the bank when the Small Business Administration helped him obtain a startup loan. Since that time, Tamara Andrews, his personal account representative at the bank, has helped him establish an automated record keeping system and advised him on payroll taxes and other federal and state regulations. She also has suggested several safe investments that will earn a higher rate of return on his deposits than a typical savings account. Why should a person starting a new business seek financial advice from a bank or other financial institution?

DEPOSITS AND SAVINGS

A company should deposit cash that isn't being used in some type of savings plan at a financial institution. The deposit offers security for the money and the opportunity to earn interest. If the business needs to have immediate access to some of its money, that money usually will be placed in a demand deposit. A **demand deposit** is money that can be withdrawn at any time with no financial penalty. To make withdrawal of the money easy, most businesses keep some money in a checking account, one type of demand deposit. Whenever money is needed for business operations, the business can issue a check, which the bank then pays from the money previously deposited. Demand deposits usually pay a very low rate of interest.

Other types of savings choices are available that offer higher interest rates. However, they either have a higher risk associated with the investment or the depositor does not have immediate access to the money deposited.

Type of Savings	Description
Regular Savings Account	A demand account that pays a low interest rate
Certificate of Deposit	Requires a minimum amount saved for a specific period of time (3 months to 5 years). Pays a fixed rate of interest that is higher for a longer savings period.
Money Market Account	Savings are invested in government securities. A minimum amount must be invested (often $500) and the interest rate can go up or down.
Treasury Instruments	Sold by the U.S government for time periods of a few months to 30 years in amounts of $1,000 to $1 million.

LOANS

Sometimes a business does not have enough cash on hand to pay current expenses. At other times, a business may need to make a very expensive purchase for land, a building, or a piece of equipment. It will need to obtain a loan from a bank or other financial institution. A **loan** is money borrowed for a specific period of time on which interest must be paid.

A business will not be able to borrow money unless evidence can be provided that it will be able to repay the loan. Most business loans are secured loans, where the business pledges property it owns that has a greater value than the amount borrowed. If the loan is not repaid, the lending company takes ownership of that property.

Two common types of business loans are a line of credit and a mortgage. A *line of credit* is an amount of money agreed upon by the lender that the business can access whenever needed. The business can write a check on the line of credit when funds are needed and then repay the amount borrowed and the interest when cash is received from customers. Money from a line of credit may be borrowed for only a few weeks or months before being repaid but remains available to the business. A *mortgage* is a long-term loan, often for 20 or 30 years, obtained to purchase land or buildings. The lender keeps title to the property until the loan is completely paid.

INVESTMENTS

Savings plans allow businesses to earn interest on the money deposited with very little risk that the money will be lost. Because of the low risk, the interest rate also is quite low. Businesses may want to earn a higher interest rate and are willing to take a higher risk that some or all of the money may be lost. Financial institutions and other businesses such as stockbrokers can assist with those investment decisions.

One type of investment that has a lower level of risk is *bonds*. Bonds are issued by businesses, organizations such as school districts or universities, and governments. Bondholders receive a specific rate of interest for the length of the bond and receive payment before stockholders and some creditors if the business or organization fails.

The best known type of investment is *stocks*, with which a business purchases ownership in another company. This type of investment is risky because it depends on the success of the company to increase the value of the stock and to pay dividends. Rather than investing in one company, money can be invested in a mutual fund. A *mutual fund* pools the money of many investors to make stock purchases in many companies. A well-managed mutual fund is usually less risky than purchasing the stock of one company.

CHECKPOINT

What are three common types of financial services used by businesses?

_____

_____

TECH TALK

BANKS AND TECHNOLOGY Banks and other companies providing financial services are increasing their use of technology to deliver services. Consumers today can complete the following activities using their home computer.

- Pay bills
- Check account balances
- Obtain a credit card or loan
- Compare the cost of buying versus leasing an automobile
- Buy and sell stocks and mutual funds
- Transfer funds from one bank account to another
- File federal and state taxes

THINK CRITICALLY What additional financial services are available on the Internet?

Businesses have many choices of financial institutions when they need financial services. Discuss with your classmates reasons why a business should work with only one bank for all of its financial needs. Then discuss reasons for working with several institutions. At the end of the discussion vote on which choice the class thinks is best.

TYPES OF FINANCIAL INSTITUTIONS

Managers work with financial institutions to obtain and manage the money a business needs. The most common type of financial institution is a bank. However many other types of businesses also provide financial services for businesses and individuals. Competition among the businesses offering those services is increasing. This competition results in the development of new products and better service. Businesspeople and consumers must be well informed and careful in selecting the financial institutions they will use.

BANKS

Businesses and consumers usually work with a bank for regular financial services. **Banks** are financial institutions regulated by state or federal governments that offer loan and deposit services for individuals and businesses. The types of services offered by a bank are expanding rapidly as customers have more choices of financial institutions. However, the most important services are to provide short- and long-term loans so businesses can finance their operations and to accept deposits so the business's money is secure and can earn interest while it is not being used.

Banks are classified by the primary types of services they provide. *Savings banks* or *savings and loan associations* specialize in a variety of savings accounts and offer consumer loans such as home loans and mortgages. A *commercial bank* offers a wide variety of services but specializes in meeting financial needs of businesses. Services include handling deposits, making loans, offering lines of credit, managing payroll, and offering tax and legal advice.

OTHER FINANCIAL ORGANIZATIONS

Changes in laws in the last part of the twentieth century encouraged other institutions to compete with banks and offer a variety of financial services. Many of those institutions emphasize investment opportunities but may also provide more common services such as loans, credit cards, and financial advice. Stock brokerage firms assist customers in buying and selling stocks. Many accept deposits of cash from their customers for which they pay competitive interest rates and allow customers to write checks on those deposits. In addition to selling insurance policies, most insurance companies provide investment services, loans, and financial advice. Investment companies and financial advisors help individuals and businesses develop financial plans. They may provide financial services or cooperate with other companies who offer those services to make sure their customers' financial needs are met.

Identify several types of businesses that offer financial services.

_____

_____

THINK CRITICALLY

1. Why should a new business owner determine the financial services the business will need before the business is actually started?

_____

_____

_____

_____

2. Why would a business select a savings plan that pays a lower interest rate than could be received from other plans?

_____

_____

_____

3. Why might a large company want to employ a person to make all investment decisions rather than using a financial services company?

_____

_____

_____

MAKE CONNECTIONS

4. BANKING Use your local newspaper or other information sources to determine current rates banks in your community are paying for various savings plans. Then use the Internet to find the rates paid by banks in other cities and states. Prepare a table that illustrates the information you gathered.

5. BUSINESS LAW State and federal governments have passed laws requiring that certain information be provided to consumers when they borrow money. Locate advertisements that offer loans to consumers for purchases of automobiles, furniture, or other expensive purchases. Read the detailed information that describes the terms of the loan. Present your advertisement to your classmates. Discuss whether the information is understandable or not and whether it helps consumers make better borrowing decisions.

6. ETHICS Often people who are least able to pay are charged the highest interest rates for loans. The businesses making the loans justify the higher rates by saying the loans are risky and many will not be repaid. Write a paragraph stating reasons supporting that practice. Then write a second paragraph stating reasons opposing that practice. Decide through a discussion with other students how businesses should set the interest rates they charge for loans.

_____

_____

_____

_____

_____

LESSON 5.3
FINANCIAL RECORDS

GOALS

DESCRIBE the importance of financial records for businesses

IDENTIFY financial records commonly used by managers

THE NEED FOR FINANCIAL RECORDS

Businesses cannot continue to operate without making a profit. Profits occur when income exceeds expenses as shown in a basic accounting equation.

$$\text{Income} - \text{Expenses} = \text{Profit}$$

Managers need to be able to determine if specific business activities are profitable and if the entire business is making a profit. They use financial records to obtain the information they need. All business managers need to understand common financial statements to make effective decisions.

Financial records are organized summaries of a business's financial activities. The records are prepared and maintained by people with skills in accounting and finance such as bookkeepers and accountants. These people follow specific procedures, rules, and even laws in preparing financial records so that the information will be reliable.

ON THE $CENE

Jonathan hung up the telephone following a short conversation with Eve, his manager. Eve said she was concerned about the financial condition of the company. While sales were increasing, the accounts payable were also increasing and the amount of cash available to the company was very low. Jonathan was not sure how the business could have financial problems if sales were increasing. What are some things that could be happening in the business that would explain Eve's concern?

USE FINANCIAL RECORDS IN BUSINESS

In the long run, financial strength of a business is determined by its *capital*, the financial resources used to operate a business. In the short run, the business needs enough cash to be able to pay its expenses. It also needs to be able to make a profit to increase its financial strength. A financially strong business is able to spend the money needed to maintain and improve operations. A successful company will be more attractive to customers, to potential investors and stockholders, and to financial institutions.

Because success is judged in dollar terms, managers must have access to accurate records and financial reports, interpret the financial information in the reports, and make decisions that will affect future financial results. Managers use financial records to

■ Understand the sources and amounts of income

■ Identify the types and amounts of expenses

■ Determine the kinds and values of assets owned by the business

■ Prepare necessary reports

■ Check on the progress and plan the future direction of the business

IMPORTANT FINANCIAL REPORTS

Financial reports are regularly prepared summaries of specific financial information for an identified period of time. Three financial reports used frequently by managers are cash flow, working capital, and financial ratios.

A *cash flow report* describes the movement of cash into and out of a business. Cash comes into a business when sales are made or when customers who buy on credit make payments. Cash goes out of a business when purchases are made or payments are made on loans or other credit purchases. Managers need to know if cash is available to make planned purchases. If adequate cash is not available, a purchase will have to be delayed or credit will have to be used. This adds to the business's expenses.

A *working capital report* shows the difference between current assets and current liabilities. The term "current" identifies assets that quickly can be converted to cash if needed and liabilities that must be paid in less than a year. Businesses need assets to be able to pay their liabilities. Higher working capital means the business is stronger financially because it will be able to pay its expenses when scheduled.

Financial ratios compare important financial information to identify possible problems. Managers examine financial ratios to determine if the financial condition of the business is improving or not. They can also compare the financial performance of their company with that of other companies using those ratios. Three important financial ratios are the following.

1. **Return on Sales** Shows how profitable specific sales have been.

2. **Inventory Turnover** Shows whether there are too many or too few products for sale.

3. **Return on Investment** Shows the rate of return the owners are receiving on the money they invested.

BUSINESS MATH CONNECTION

Calculate return on sales, inventory turnover, and return on investment for a business, assuming a net profit of $150,000, sales of $1,200,000, cost of goods sold of $400,000, average inventory of $120,000, and total assets of $600,000.

Return on sales = Net profit ÷ Sales

Inventory turnover = Cost of goods sold ÷ Average inventory

Return on investment = Net profit ÷ Total assets

SOLUTION

Return on sales = $150,000 ÷ $1,200,000 = 0.125 = 12.5%

Inventory turnover = $400,000 ÷ $120,000 = 3.33

Return on investment = $150,000 ÷ $600,000 = 0.25 = 25%

THINK CRITICALLY Do you think each of the ratios above indicate a strong financial performance? Why or why not?

CHECKPOINT ✓

How can financial records and reports help a business manager make better decisions?

_____

_____

IMPORTANT FINANCIAL RECORDS

Businesses are required to maintain financial records to prepare taxes and other government reports. Managers and owners use those records to determine the company's financial position. Financial records used by businesses include records of assets, receipts, payments, and payroll.

ASSET RECORDS

A business uses a number of resources in its operations. The resources owned by a business are its *assets*. The business needs to keep complete records of its assets and their value. The value of some assets, such as land and buildings, may increase over time. Other assets such as equipment, materials, and supplies usually lose value as they get older. If an asset increases in value, the company's financial position improves. If assets lose their value, they will have to be replaced which is a cost to the business. Asset records show each asset of the business, its original and current value, and any amount the company owes on the asset.

RECEIPTS AND PAYMENTS RECORDS

Most businesses buy and sell using both cash and credit. This requires three types of records to be maintained, including cash records, accounts receivable, and accounts payable.

Cash records report both cash receipts and cash payments. You may have a checking account. The checkbook record you maintain is an example of a cash record. A cash record reports every time cash is received including the date, the amount, the source of the payment, and its purpose. Also any cash payment made by the business is recorded in detail. The cash balance identifies how much cash is available at a specific time.

When credit is used, accounts receivable and accounts payable records are needed. *Accounts payable* record all credit purchases made by the business. *Accounts receivable* maintain a record of all credit sales. Each type of record needs to include the name of the company or individual who owes or is owed money, what was purchased or sold, the date, amount, payments as they are made, and the current account balance. Each type of record should be reviewed regularly to insure payments are up-to-date.

In small groups, identify ways that financial records can help a manager improve the financial condition of a business. Focus on cash, assets, expenses, and the use of credit.

PAYROLL RECORDS

Businesses must keep complete records of all employees. They are needed to make quarterly reports and payments to the state and federal government. They also are used to track how much the business spends on salaries and wages to produce and sell its products and services. Each part-time and full-time employee has an individual record. The record identifies the employee, date of employment, job category, and rate of pay. It reports the total salary or wage paid to date and the type and cost of all employee benefits. That includes amounts withheld for taxes, social security, Medicare, and insurance.

BUDGETS

Financial records and reports help managers understand what has happened in the business. They also are used to prepare budgets. A **budget** is a specific, written financial plan. Budgets are prepared for a specific period of time such as a month, six months, or a year. Records of past financial performance are used to prepare budgets.

Managers develop budgets to estimate financial performance. They then use the budget to compare actual performance during the time for which the budget was prepared. If actual performance differs from the budget, the manager can identify if the business is doing better than expected or if a problem exists that needs attention. Common types of business budgets include production, sales, expenses, purchases, and cash budgets.

What are the important types of financial records needed by businesses?

_____

_____

THINK CRITICALLY

1. Why do managers need to be concerned about both income and expenses when making financial decisions?

_____

_____

_____

2. Why is the amount of cash available in a business important information for a manager?

_____

_____

_____

3. In addition to managers, who else might need to have the information contained in the financial records of a business?

_____

_____

_____

4. How do the financial records of a business help managers prepare budgets?

_____

_____

_____

MAKE CONNECTIONS

5. PERSONAL FINANCE Individuals use several tools to manage their finances. They receive money in the form of cash and checks. They make payment with cash, checks, credit cards, and debit cards. You are the personal financial consultant to someone who uses all of those tools. What records do you think the person should maintain? How should they use each type of record to make sure they are managing their finances effectively? Use word processing software to write a paragraph answering these questions.

6. BUSINESS MATH Calculate each of the following financial ratios using the information provided. Use spreadsheet software to calculate your answers.

Ratio	Financial Information	Answer
Return on sales	Net profit = $33,800 Sales = $626,600	
Inventory turnover	Cost of goods sold = $8,265,000 Average inventory = $1,325,500	
Return on investment	Net profit = $320,000 Total assets = $6,500,100	

LESSON 5.4
CREDIT AND INSURANCE

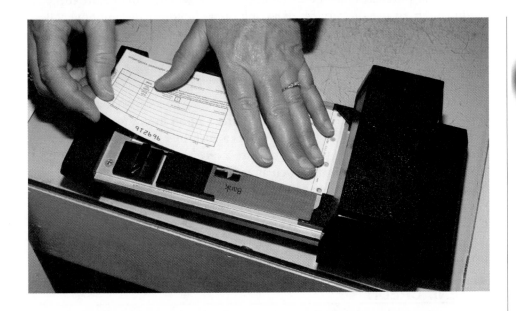

DESCRIBE how businesses use credit effectively

UNDERSTAND the need to manage risk in business with and without insurance

EXTEND AND RECEIVE CREDIT

Use of credit in the U.S. economy is very common. It is difficult to consider what consumers would do without credit cards and the ability to purchase on credit. Businesses also would have a difficult time operating without the use of credit. Businesses use credit when they make purchases and extend credit to customers to increase the volume of their sales.

Both consumers and businesses must use credit carefully. Many consumers make so many purchases on credit they are unable to keep up with the payments. That results in high interest charges and ultimately credit problems. Businesses that extend credit to consumers who will not be able to pay do not receive money for the products they have sold. This means the business will not make a profit and may be unable to pay its own bills.

ON THE $CENE

Bountiful Bed and Breakfast is a popular family-run hotel and restaurant. But the worst has just happened. A fire in the kitchen resulted in water and smoke damage throughout the building. Bountiful would have to close for renovations for at least two months right at the beginning of the busy tourist season. Owners Jack and Judy Tomlesh are uncertain whether they have enough money to pay for repairs, in addition to the many continuing expenses, while the business is closed. They are meeting with their accountant and insurance agent to determine what to do. What questions should the couple be prepared to ask?

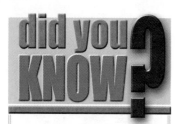

TYPES OF CREDIT

Before extending credit to consumers or other businesses, a business must establish credit policies. Those policies include such things as who will receive credit, what purchases may be made using credit, whether to operate the credit system or use the services of a bank or credit company, and how collections will be made. An important decision is the type of credit to offer.

Installment Credit When people borrow money to pay for major purchases such as automobiles or furniture, home improvements, education, or a vacation, they usually use *installment credit*. With installment credit, the purchaser signs an agreement to make a specific number of payments for a certain number of months or years at an agreed-upon interest rate.

Revolving Credit If a business wants a customer to be able to make purchases on credit at any time, it may use a *revolving credit plan*. With revolving credit, customers are given a credit limit and can make purchases on credit at any time as long as the total amount doesn't exceed that limit.

Credit Cards Credit cards are a form of revolving credit. The credit card system can be owned by the business. However, most businesses use a company such as MasterCard, Visa, or American Express. The business pays a fee to the credit company, normally a small percentage of the credit sales.

EXTEND CREDIT

Businesses must be careful in extending credit. A customer's creditworthiness determines if credit can be extended and the credit terms that will be offered. **Creditworthiness** is a person's capability to pay for credit. Several factors make up creditworthiness. They are often called the four Cs of credit.

Character Character judges whether a person is a responsible consumer and manages money well. A person who has a poor credit record or does not make payments on time will not have a high character rating.

Capacity Capacity determines whether a person has the income and other financial resources to be able to make the necessary payments. To determine capacity, a business needs to know the person's income, employment history, amount of savings, monthly expenses, and current credit payments.

Capital Capital is a measure of the person's financial worth. People with more assets than liabilities will have a higher capital rating. Capital is important for large loans that must be paid over a number of years because it means the consumer will be able to pay for credit even if there are short-term problems with monthly income, such as losing or changing jobs.

Conditions The final C of credit judges the economic conditions facing the business and its customers. If the economy is healthy, a business is more likely to extend credit. During conditions of increasing unemployment or increasing interest rates, businesses will be much more cautious.

CHECKPOINT

What factors determine a person's creditworthiness?

_____

_____

INSURE BUSINESS RISKS

You face risks every day. Those risks include accidents, illness, or financial problems. If you are careful and aware of possible risks, you can avoid most of them. Businesses also face risks that may result in problems or even failure. Businesspeople must make careful plans to avoid risk or to be able to reduce damage from problems that occur. Purchasing insurance is one way businesses manage risk. **Insurance** limits the amount of financial loss from an uncontrollable event in exchange for a regular payment of money.

HOW INSURANCE WORKS

Every business faces losses from fire, theft, injury of employees or customers, accidents that cause damage to vehicles and property, and many other problems. It is impossible to determine whether any or all of those losses will occur to a specific business, when they will occur, or the amount of loss that will result.

When thousands of businesses face the same types of risks, it is possible to accurately predict the type and amount of losses that will occur among all of those businesses in a certain period of time. The prediction can be made if records of losses are kept for many years.

Insurance companies keep those records and make predictions of losses that businesses face. Based on those records, the insurance company sells insurance to businesses to protect them from a major financial loss. The cost of insurance is determined by the number of businesses insured and the amount the insurance company predicts it will have to pay for losses suffered by those businesses during the year.

UNDERSTAND INSURANCE

Specific terms are used when purchasing insurance. Important insurance terms are listed and defined in the box on the next page. Businesses insure against a number of perils. Typically, a business will purchase property insurance, vehicle insurance, liability insurance, and insurance on people.

Property Insurance The buildings, equipment, and product of a business are needed in order to operate. They may suffer damage from several perils. Businesses purchase fire insurance to cover the cost of repairing or replacing property damaged in a fire. If property is stolen or damaged by burglars, employees, or customers, insurance will help cover the losses. Sometimes products are lost or damaged while being transported from the business to the customer's location. Insurance carried by the business or the transportation company can provide protection against that loss.

Vehicle Insurance The cars, trucks, and other vehicles owned or leased by a business will usually be insured. Vehicle insurance covers costs of repairing or replacing vehicles involved in accidents. It also will pay for damage to property caused by a company's vehicle and for medical expenses of people who are injured in an accident involving the vehicles.

In small groups, identify ways that a business can reduce the amount of losses from the following perils: fire, vehicle accidents, liability for damage caused by its products, and employee illness and accidents.

Common Insurance Terms

Policy	Written contract between insurer and policyholder
Insurer	Company who sells insurance, collects premiums, and pays for losses suffered by policyholder
Policyholder	Person or company purchasing insurance
Premium	Payment by policyholder to insurer for protection against a loss
Insurance Rate	Amount the insurance company charges for a specified amount of insurance
Peril	Cause of a loss
Risk	Uncertainty that a loss will occur
Insurable Interest	Possibility that a person or company may suffer financial loss if the people or property to be insured are harmed

Liability Insurance A business may be sued if one of its products causes damage or injury. If an employee or customer is injured while in the business, the company may be financially liable. Professionals like doctors and lawyers may be sued for malpractice if a patient or client feels the person did not provide appropriate care or advice. If an employee does something that results in harm to customers or others, the company may be sued. Liability insurance offers protection against those types of losses.

Insurance on People Because employees and managers are important to a company's success, injuries, illness, or death of those people may result in financial losses. Three types of insurance are commonly provided for the people in a business. *Health insurance* pays some or all of the cost of medical care for employees. *Disability insurance* provides money to employees who cannot work for an extended time due to accidents or illness. *Life insurance* offers compensation in the event of the death of the insured.

MANAGE RISK

Businesses cannot insure against every type of risk. Some risks cannot be anticipated, or the cost of insurance may be so high the business cannot afford the premiums. Managers and employees attempt to identify possible risks and reduce the chances that it will happen. Employees are taught safe operating procedures and equipment is maintained to prevent injuries. Aisles and walkways are kept clear. Spills are immediately cleaned. Products are carefully stored so employees and customers are not hurt. Special security precautions are taken to reduce employee theft, burglary, and shoplifting.

Some product liability lawsuits against companies for injuries suffered by consumers have resulted in settlements of hundreds of millions of dollars. Some companies have gone out of business as a result. Lawmakers in several states have proposed legislation to place a cap of a million dollars or less on the amount of money a company has to pay in such cases. Write a one-page paper in support of or opposing that legislation. Support your opinion with specific reasons.

What types of insurance should businesses consider purchasing?

_____

_____

THINK CRITICALLY

1. What affect will the decision to not offer credit to customers have on a business?

_____

_____

_____

2. What steps can a person take to improve each of the four Cs of credit?

_____

_____

_____

_____

3. Why is it important for insurance companies to keep insurance premiums as low as possible?

_____

_____

_____

4. What are some examples of business risks that usually cannot be insured because they cannot be predicted?

_____

_____

_____

MAKE CONNECTIONS

5. TECHNOLOGY Use the Internet to locate a web site that compares the interest rates and annual fees charged to consumers for credit cards. List the three most inexpensive and the three most expensive credit cards.

_____

_____

6. BUSINESS MATH A basic example of how insurance companies calculate the rates they charge for property insurance is shown by the following formula

Total amount of ÷ Total value of all × 1,000 = Rate per $1,000
predicted losses   property insured   of property

Using spreadsheet software, calculate the insurance rates for each of the following values:

Predicted losses	Total property value	Insurance rate
$10,500	$550,000	
$230,600	$1,960,900	
$1,820,750	$55,275,000	

REVIEW

CHAPTER SUMMARY

LESSON 5.1 Finance a Business

A. The financial strength of a business is one of the most important factors to its success. Many businesses fail due to poor financial management.

B. When deciding on financing the important factors to consider are ownership, the cost of financing, and financing requirements.

LESSON 5.2 Financial Services

A. A business must manage its money wisely. Owners and managers are responsible for financial decisions. All businesses use the services of financial institutions.

B. Managers work with financial institutions to obtain and manage the money a business needs.

LESSON 5.3 Financial Records

A. Specific procedures, rules, and even laws must be followed in maintaining financial records so the records will be reliable.

B. Several important financial records are used by all businesses, including records of assets, receipts, payments, and payroll.

LESSON 5.4 Credit and Insurance

A. Businesses use credit when they make purchases and extend credit to customers to increase the volume of their sales.

B. Businesspeople must make careful plans to avoid risk or to be able to reduce the damage resulting from problems that occur.

VOCABULARY BUILDER

Choose the term that best fits the definition. Write the letter of the answer in the space provided. Some terms may not be used.

_____ **1.** Organized summaries of a business's financial activities

_____ **2.** Limits the amount of financial loss from an uncontrollable event in exchange for a regular payment of money

_____ **3.** Money put in a financial institution that can be withdrawn at any time with no financial penalty

_____ **4.** A specific, written financial plan

_____ **5.** Money obtained from sources other than business owners

_____ **6.** Money borrowed for a specific period of time on which interest must be paid

_____ **7.** The financial resources used to operate a business

_____ **8.** A person's ability to pay for credit extended

_____ **9.** Financial resources provided by the owners of a business

_____ **10.** Financial institutions regulated by state or federal governments that offer loan and deposit services

a. banks

b. budget

c. capital

d. credit-worthiness

e. debt capital

f. demand deposit

g. equity capital

h. financial records

i. insurance

j. loan

CHAPTER 5

REVIEW CONCEPTS

11. What is the most common form of debt capital for a business?

_____

_____

_____

POINT YOUR
BROWSER

b2000.swep.com

12. What are three important factors to consider when deciding on financing a business?

_____

_____

_____

_____

13. Identify the types of financial services offered to businesses by financial institutions.

_____

_____

_____

_____

14. How did changes in laws in the last part of the twentieth century affect banks?

_____

_____

_____

_____

15. What are several specific ways that managers use financial records?

_____

_____

_____

_____

16. What is the relationship between a budget and the actual financial performance of a business?

_____

_____

_____

_____

_____

17. Identify three types of credit offered by businesses.

_____

_____

18. How do insurance companies determine the amount to charge for insurance?

_____

_____

_____

_____

APPLY WHAT YOU LEARNED

19. Why are stockholders considered owners of the business in which they have purchased stock?

_____

_____

_____

_____

20. Why might a business borrow money even though it has cash available as well as money in a savings and checking account?

_____

_____

_____

_____

21. What should a business do if it finds that customers who owe money are not keeping their payments up to date?

_____

_____

_____

_____

22. Why would a company want to purchase life insurance that pays money to the company in the event an owner or top executive dies?

_____

_____

_____

_____

CHAPTER 5

MAKE CONNECTIONS

23. ETHICS Many credit card companies send credit cards to people without checking their creditworthiness carefully. They hope the people will use the credit card, not pay off the balance, and then pay a high rate of interest on the balance. What is your view of that practice? How can consumers protect themselves against the practice? Should state or federal governments regulate that practice? Why or why not? Prepare to give a class presentation on this topic.

24. PERSONAL FINANCE Prepare a personal budget for one month using spreadsheet software. List the sources and anticipated amounts of income you will receive during the month. Then identify the major categories of expenses you will have and predict the amount you will spend in each category. After you have completed the budget, carefully track your income and expenses for one week and compare it to your budget. Write a brief statement describing how the budget compares to your actual financial performance.

_____

_____

_____

_____

_____

_____

25. BUSINESS COMMUNICATION You are the financial manager for the Action Company. One of your best customers, Jeb Yarcho, has fallen behind in making payments on the revolving credit account you have established for him. He has not made any payments for two months and has added an additional $500 of charges during that time. Using word processing sofware, write a letter requesting payment and offering to help if necessary. Make the letter positive, while communicating the serious nature of the problem.

26. TECHNOLOGY Use the Internet to find a web site that has a loan calculator. A loan calculator allows you to enter the amount of a loan, the length of the loan in months or years, and the interest rate. It will then calculate a monthly payment and the total amount of interest that must be paid during the time of the loan. Using the loan calculator, determine the monthly payment and total interest paid for different interest rates if $25,000 is borrowed for 5 years.

_____

_____

_____

_____

_____

SPHERION

Spherion began in 1946 by placing employees in temporary positions. Today it is a worldwide human resources management company that provides a broad range of services assisting companies to recruit, hire, train, and manage employees. Spherion is headquartered in Ft. Lauderdale, Florida, and has more than 1,000 offices in North America, Europe, Australia, and Asia. It is the fifth largest private employer in the United States.

A Temporary Staffing Career Agent at Spherion recruits new employees for other companies. The Career Agent gives skill tests, arranges training, and provides coaching and counseling for the temporary employees to make sure they are satisfied with their work. To qualify as a Career Agent, you need a college degree or the equivalent in work experience. You need to be flexible and have excellent computer and financial skills. You need strong human relations and communications abilities to meet employer and employee needs and solve problems.

THINK CRITICALLY

1. Why would a company use an employment agency rather than do its own hiring?
2. What are the advantages and disadvantages of a temporary position?

MANAGE HUMAN RESOURCES

LESSONS

6.1 HRM ACTIVITIES

6.2 RECRUIT AND HIRE

6.3 MANAGE PERFORMANCE

6.4 TRAIN AND DEVELOP

The Chapter 6 video for this module introduces the concepts in this chapter.

PROJECT
Improve Employee Performance

PROJECT OBJECTIVES

■ Identify how employee needs are satisfied by human resources activities
■ Describe procedures for recruiting and hiring new employees
■ Develop procedures to manage employee performance
■ Discuss how to provide employee training

GETTING STARTED

Read through the Project Process below. Make a list of any materials and information you will need and decide how you will get them.

PROJECT PROCESS

Part 1 LESSON 6.1 Identify at least five needs individuals are attempting to satisfy through employment. Then describe ways an employer can satisfy each of the needs.

Part 2 LESSON 6.2 In small groups, brainstorm ways that businesses can identify and recruit new employees. Make a list of steps the employer will need to take in order to identify and hire the best of these employees.

Part 3 LESSON 6.3 With a partner, develop two short role-plays in which an employee and manager discuss the employee's performance. The role-plays should illustrate both ineffective and effective discussions.

Part 4 LESSON 6.4 You are responsible for helping a new employee become familiar with the company and a new job. Discuss how you would organize a short training program for the person's first day on the job.

CHAPTER REVIEW

Project Wrap-up Locate and visit web sites from several companies that have been identified as "the best places to work in the U.S." Then make a list of things they do for employees that have resulted in the recognition as a good employer.

LESSON 6.1
HRM ACTIVITIES

RECOGNIZE the importance of human resources to businesses

IDENTIFY important services provided by human resources

THE IMPORTANCE OF PEOPLE

Employees are responsible for the success of a business. They determine whether the work is performed correctly or if there are errors that lead to wasted materials and defective products. When customers have questions or problems, employees must answer the questions and solve the problems. If they do that well, customers will be satisfied and will continue to buy from the company.

Human resources is another name for employees. All managers work with human resources. However a specific type of management is known as human resources management. **Human resources management (HRM) is** all of the activities involved with hiring, training, and compensating the people who work for a company. Employees' pay, training, benefits, work environment, and many other factors contribute to their motivation, ability, and willingness to do a good job. The people who work in human resources management perform the tasks that help the company develop skilled, productive, and satisfied employees.

ON THE $CENE

Sangi Desh showed up for his first day of work fifteen minutes early at 7:45 a.m. Sangi was excited about the new job and wanted to do well. He was unsure of what would happen during his first day but had many questions. The company had given a large employee handbook to him when he accepted the job offer. But it had so much information, it left him confused. He wasn't sure how to get answers to his questions. What could the company do to help Sangi feel welcome and confident?

HIRE THE RIGHT PEOPLE

As jobs become more complex and require people with a high level of knowledge and skill, businesses are challenged with finding the right person for each job. Businesses often have to compete with each other for highly skilled employees. They must offer a good wage or salary and benefits to attract and keep those employees. Because those skilled employees are costly, the company needs to make sure the right people are hired.

The first requirement is that the employee has the necessary knowledge and skill to complete the work. Next the employee must have a good work ethic and want to do the work. Because much work in businesses requires teamwork, employees must also be able to work well with each other. Because jobs are constantly changing, employees need to be interested in improving their skills by attending training and completing additional education.

KEEP EMPLOYEES SATISFIED

Once a company is able to hire the employees it needs, it is important to keep them. One company estimated that it costs more than $20,000 to replace an employee who leaves. That cost includes recruiting a new employee, providing training, and the productivity loss that occurs from the time one person leaves until the new employee is hired and performing as well as the former employee. The cost to replace employees with very specialized skills or managers may be as high as $100,000. Controlling the amount of employee turnover is an important management responsibility. *Employee turnover* is the rate at which employees leave the business. Businesses track the turnover rate and report it to each manager. If the turnover rate is higher in some departments than others or if the rate is increasing, managers will be expected to find ways to reduce the rate.

The wages or salary and benefits an employee receives certainly contribute to employee satisfaction. However, most employee surveys suggest that other things are even more important. People want interesting work that uses their skills. They want to be recognized and valued for the work they do. Being involved in decisions, having responsibility, and career advancement opportunities also are important. Many things that make employees satisfied with their work do not cost a great deal of money. They do require that managers be aware of employee needs and help them feel they are an important part of the company.

If a company's average employment during June was 840 and 36 people left during the month, what is the employee turnover rate?

SOLUTION
The formula used is

$$\text{Employee turnover rate} = \frac{\text{Number of employees leaving during one month}}{\text{Average number of employees during the month}}$$

$$\text{Employee turnover rate} = \frac{36}{840} = 0.0429 = 4.29\%$$

CHECKPOINT ✓

Define human resources management.

_____

_____

THE ROLE OF HUMAN RESOURCES

Help Wanted

Human resources management is a very complex part of business operations. Many laws and regulations must be understood and followed when people are hired, paid, promoted, reprimanded, or terminated. Records must be prepared and maintained. Employee questions about salaries and benefits, education and training opportunities, taxes, vacations, and retirement need to be answered. Managers need help with hiring new employees, evaluating performance, and handling employee problems.

Most companies have a department responsible for human resources management. Large companies may have several specialized divisions within the department, each of which deals with a specific area in human resources. Human resources (often called HR) is a service department. It provides services for employees and managers in other departments in the company.

PROVIDE SERVICES

Employment The employment function of human resources involves all activities required to maintain an adequate number of qualified employees for the company. These include determining hiring needs, recruiting applicants, determining qualifications of applicants, and hiring the most qualified to fill available jobs. Job changes such as transfers, promotions, retirements, dismissals, also are included in the employment function.

Wages and Benefits HR is typically responsible for developing a pay system that classifies jobs according to levels and pay ranges. When a person is hired, promoted, or given a pay increase, HR helps ensure that the employee is paid the correct amount. Companies offer benefits to their employees in addition to wages. Some benefits, such as social security and Medicare, are required by law. Others, such as insurance and vacations, are not legally required, but many companies provide them. HR employees study what benefits can be offered, determine the cost of each benefit, and help management develop the benefits plan. They provide information to employees about each benefit and help employees recognize the value of their benefits.

Performance Improvement Performance improvement involves training and educating employees to insure high quality and efficient work. New employees receive an orientation to the company and initial training to make sure they are successful in the new job. After their initial training, employees must be prepared for changes in equipment or procedures as well as for promotions and job transfers.

Employee Relations HR plays a major role in employee relations by insuring effective communication and cooperation throughout the company. If a labor union is organized within a company, a very formal set of relationships exists between employees and management. HR specialists assist in negotiating the contract with the union and deal with employee problems that relate to the contract. If there is no union, HR specialists perform the same type of activities, but usually in a less formal way. HR assures that the company complies with all equal employment and affirmative action laws.

Health and Safety Illnesses and injuries among employees are expensive for companies. The HR department is responsible for maintaining safe work areas and work procedures, enforcing laws and regulations related to safety and health, and providing adequate education and training in health and safety. Most HR departments provide regular safety training, place safety posters and materials in the work place to remind workers to follow safety procedures, and help identify and correct possible safety problems. They also collect and report data on injuries and illnesses to be sure everyone is well informed about the level of safety in the company.

Performance Management Individual managers are responsible for evaluating the employees they supervise and using the results to improve performance. The role of HR in performance management is to develop the evaluation system and materials and educate managers and employees on the proper methods for evaluating and improving performance. They also maintain the results of the evaluations in each employee's personnel file.

Employee Assistance Programs Employee assistance programs (EAPs) provide confidential personal problem-solving, counseling, and support services for employees. Some programs provide special services for working families such as day care or elder care, or help to arrange car-pooling. Businesses have found that when employees are able to deal effectively with personal problems they are more effective at work.

List all of the human resources services on a sheet of paper. Then rank them from 1 to 7, with 1 as most important, in the order you think employees value the services. Rank them again in the order of importance to the company. Compare your rankings with other students.

IMPROVE SERVICES

Companies are looking at ways to improve HR services while controlling the costs of those services. They are finding many ways to use technology to streamline work and reduce paperwork. Computers are used to gather and store employment information making access and updates easy. When an employee gets a pay increase or has a new address, HR employees can easily change computer records. The Internet also is changing the way human resources services are provided. Companies can use e-mail to quickly communicate new policies or benefit options to all employees. Surveys and evaluation forms can be completed online. Employees can log on to the company web site to check on benefits and other employment information.

What are the common services provided by human resources departments?

137

THINK CRITICALLY

1. Why should companies try to keep employees who work for them?

_____

_____

_____

2. Name at least three things companies do that might cause employees to become dissatisfied.

_____

_____

_____

3. Why do companies have human resources departments instead of making each manager responsible for those services?

_____

_____

_____

4. What concerns should a company and employees have about using the Internet to provide human resources information?

_____

_____

_____

MAKE CONNECTIONS

5. TECHNOLOGY Locate a company that allows people to apply for jobs using the Internet. Identify the steps that are required to make an application and the information that is requested by the company.

_____

_____

_____

_____

6. RESEARCH Develop a questionnaire that asks respondents to identify the factors that they think would make a business one of the top places to work in the United States. Use the questionnaire to survey 10 people. Summarize your results and develop a chart or graph to illustrate them. Present an oral report using the survey and illustration.

_____

_____

_____

_____

_____

LESSON 6.2
RECRUIT AND HIRE

RECRUIT NEW EMPLOYEES

One of the most important management activities is hiring new employees. When a person is hired with the skills that match the job opening, the work will likely be done well. If the new employee likes the job, the company, and coworkers, the person may continue to work for the company for a long time. Satisfied employees are not only good workers, but they often recruit others to work for the company by encouraging friends and other people they know to apply for job openings.

On the other hand, if a poor match is made between the new employee and the job, the work will not be done well and time must be spent helping the new employee learn the job or correcting errors. The employee will become frustrated and problems often will develop between the employee, the manager, and coworkers. Usually the employee will quit or be fired and the company will need to go through the recruitment process again.

ON THE $CENE

Diane Bell is sitting at her desk in the HR department looking at the applications for a job opening in the medical lab. In addition to the completed application form, she has a resume and college transcript, a list of previous jobs and employers, and the names and telephone numbers of references for each applicant. She needs to select two people to interview and knows she always learns a lot more about each person from the interview than from the application form. She finds it difficult to select the best candidates to interview. How should Ms. Bell use the application materials to select the two interviewees? What additional information would be helpful in making the decision?

IDENTIFY A JOB OPENING

The recruitment process begins when a company has a job opening. Openings occur for several reasons. Usually, a person needs to be hired as a replacement. The replacement may be needed because a current employee received a promotion or transferred to another job.

Another reason for needing a replacement is if an employee leaves the company. The employee may have been hired by another business or left due to retirement, moving from the community, attending college full-time, or other reasons. It is also possible the employee was terminated for poor performance.

Company growth will usually mean opportunities for new employees. As a company expands by adding products or entering new markets, additional employees will be added to help with the increased workload.

Companies should try to anticipate a job opening as far in advance as possible. That allows them to have a new person available to fill the opening before the current employee leaves the job or shortly after. If there is a delay in filling the position, the company may have difficulty getting all of the work completed. Other employees in the department may be asked to work overtime or a temporary employee will need to be hired.

Human resources personnel work with the manager of the department in which the job opening exists. The HR department must have detailed and accurate information about the position in order to screen applicants and choose only the most qualified people to interview. To compile the needed information, companies prepare a job description and job specification for each position in the company. A **job description** is a list of the basic tasks that make up a job. A **job specification** is a list of the qualifications a worker needs to do that job. The information is used to recruit several qualified applicants and to help determine the best candidate for the job.

SOURCES OF JOB APPLICANTS

It is usually the responsibility of the human resources department to recruit applicants for all job openings in a company. They need to use procedures that result in a reasonable number of applicants. If only a small number apply, the chances of finding someone who is well-qualified decreases. If there are too many applicants, the process of selecting the most qualified will take longer. Many sources of prospective employees exist.

Current Employees Companies should give current employees the first opportunity to apply for job openings. The chance for a new, often higher-paying job is an incentive for employees. The job may provide better work hours or a better match with the employee's interests and skills.

Employee Recommendations Current employees may recommend people they know for open positions in the company. If they are aware of job openings and requirements, they often can identify someone they know who is qualified. Because current employees like working for the company, their recommendation may encourage the person to apply.

Employment Agencies Employment agencies are businesses that actively recruit, evaluate, and help people prepare for and locate jobs. They will work with companies to publicize available jobs and to identify qualified candidates for job openings. They also work with individuals to help them obtain a job.

The Internet The Internet has become a popular resource for recruiting job applicants. Web sites such as monster.com provide thousands of job listings that job seekers can search by type of job, location, company, or salary expectations. Companies that regularly hire employees place a link to employment opportunities on their home page so that prospective employees can obtain an up-to-date listing of available jobs.

Other Sources Advertising is a common method of obtaining job applicants. Companies frequently use newspaper advertising to quickly inform people of an opening. Colleges and universities, vocational and technical schools, and an increasing number of high schools have placement offices to assist graduates in obtaining jobs. Large businesses accept unsolicited applications even if there are no current openings. The applications are reviewed for minimum qualifications and matched to job categories in the company. They are available for review as openings occur.

COMMUNICATE

An employment advertisement must be written to attract the interest of prospective employees and to provide adequate information so only qualified applicants apply. Write an employment advertisement for a job and company with which you are familiar. If needed, interview a person who holds the job to gather information for the advertisement. The advertisement should be no longer than 60 words.

CHECKPOINT

What are some common sources companies can use to recruit new employees?

_____

_____

COMPLETE THE HIRING PROCESS

Most businesses have an application form that prospective employees must complete. The form is used to obtain needed personal information about the applicant as well as education and work history. It may identify specific areas of knowledge or skill the applicant possesses as well as specialized certifications and licenses.

The application form should only ask for information necessary to make the best selection for the job. The company must be careful that the form does not ask for discriminatory or illegal information. In addition to the application form, the company may ask for a personal resume and a letter of application. The resume and letter provide opportunities for the applicant to provide a more personal perspective including reasons for interest in the job opening.

SELECTION PROCEDURES

After applications have been received, companies follow specific procedures to identify the most qualified candidates and then to select the person to whom they will make a job offer. The typical selection procedures are

1. Written applications are reviewed to eliminate people who do not meet minimum qualifications. Applicants often are eliminated because they fill out the application form incorrectly, do not provide all of the needed information, or demonstrate poor written communication skills.

2. The remaining applicants are contacted to confirm information on the application and to provide more information to the applicant about the company and the job. Often a brief initial interview is held in person or by telephone to check the person's oral communication skills.

3. Information on the application form is checked for accuracy by contacting schools attended, previous employers, and listed references. Careful questioning of a reference can often reveal important information about an applicant's strengths, work habits, and human relations skills.

4. If specific knowledge or skill is required for the job, applicants may be tested. To be legal, the tests must measure only characteristics important for success on the job.

THE HIRING DECISION

Applicants that remain after the selection procedures are ranked and the manager or an employee team from the department that has the opening interviews the top applicants. During the interview, the applicant should be provided information about the job and have an opportunity to meet the people he or she will work with. The final selection is made by comparing the information gathered with the job description and specifications. The decision should be made carefully and objectively so that the best applicant is selected. Usually the manager or HR representative contacts the applicant and makes a specific job offer including the salary and benefits.

Many businesses require prospective employees to pass a physical exam, including drug screening, before they can begin work. The HR department helps the new employee complete necessary paperwork, such as tax and insurance enrollment forms. To help the employee become comfortable with the company and the new job, an orientation program and initial training is provided. After the new employee has been at work for several weeks, the human resources department should follow up to make sure the new employee is succeeding on the job.

CHECKPOINT

What selection procedures should managers follow to identify the best-qualified person for a job opening?

_____

_____

THINK CRITICALLY

1. Why are job descriptions and job specifications so important when recruiting and hiring a new employee?

_____

_____

_____

2. What questions would you ask a previous employer to determine whether to hire an applicant?

_____

_____

_____

3. What are the benefits of using a team of employees to interview job applicants?

_____

_____

_____

4. Identify the advantages and disadvantages of using tests as a part of the selection process.

_____

_____

_____

MAKE CONNECTIONS

5. **TECHNOLOGY** Use the Internet to locate a web site that advertises job openings for many companies. Record the Internet address of the web site as well as the name of the company or organization that manages the site. Identify three jobs that interest you. From the information listed, develop a job description and job specification for each job. Share the information in class.

_____

_____

_____

6. **BUSINESS LAW** Items on job applications and questions used to interview prospective job applicants must be carefully developed so they do not ask for inappropriate or illegal information. Information can only be collected that relates specifically to an applicant's ability to perform the job successfully. Use the Internet or a library to identify examples of illegal or inappropriate questions. Focus on why the questions should not be used and how the answers could be misused when selecting the best candidate for a job opening. Prepare to present this information in class.

_____

_____

_____

LESSON 6.3
MANAGE PERFORMANCE

DESCRIBE how the work environment and motivation affect performance

UNDERSTAND how to complete a performance review

FACTORS AFFECTING PERFORMANCE

NeXers, GenXers, Baby Boomers. Those terms are used to identify demographic groups from which the current and future employees of businesses will come. The needs and expectations of individuals in each group differ from each other and from those of workers in the past.

Getting employees to complete work takes more than a supervisor giving orders. In fact, if employees think they are being told what to do without any input or involvement, they will likely not perform as well as they can.

Satisfied employees are more productive and more likely to want to stay with the company and contribute to its success. Therefore, managers spend considerable time working with employees to make the work environment as satisfying as possible. Studies have found that employees are most satisfied

ON THE $CENE

Alexia Christophe was preparing the end-of-year performance report for her department. The report summarized the overall performance of her work team, gave individual performance ratings for each employee, recommended salary increases and bonuses, and identified employees the manager felt deserved special recognition. Alexia struggled with the report. She believed all of her employees were motivated to do a good job, and each had strengths as well as areas where they could improve. What factors should Alexia consider when making salary and bonus recommendations? Should people who have the highest performance ratings receive the largest increases or bonuses? What other types of recognition could be provided to employees?

with their work when they perform interesting work, feel responsible for the work, receive recognition for good work, and have a feeling of achievement.

IMPROVE THE WORK ENVIRONMENT

A work environment in which employees are motivated to do their best is not always the one with the newest buildings or the latest equipment. In fact many companies with older but well maintained buildings and equipment are very productive. They have been successful in designing the work environment and jobs to better meet employee needs. **Job design** is the kinds of tasks that make up a job and the way workers perform these tasks in doing their jobs.

Successful organizations try to make work more meaningful and motivating for employees. One way to do this is through **job enlargement**, which is making a job more interesting by adding variety to the tasks. In the past it was believed that employees would be more efficient if they were assigned one specific task which they repeated over and over. With job enlargement, employees working in the same area are each trained to complete several tasks. They are able to help each other, share the work, or exchange work tasks from time to time. In this way they have variety in their work and more control over what they do making the work less monotonous and boring. The company benefits from having several people who can perform many tasks rather than many specialized employees who can perform only one part of a complex job.

Another way to use job design to improve employee satisfaction is to involve employees in decision making. **Job enrichment** is giving employees the authority to make meaningful decisions about their work. For example, managers may allow workers to make choices about how to schedule their work. Managers may ask employees for advice on how to improve performance or how to reduce errors. Job responsibilities may be changed so employees can solve problems themselves without having to check with their supervisor. In many companies, teams of employees are assigned the full responsibility for day-to-day operation of a work area and only call on a manager when they face a unique problem they are unable to solve.

UNDERSTAND EMPLOYEE MOTIVATION

Motivated employees like their work and are more productive. They want the business to be successful. A manager cannot directly motivate employees but can help to create a work environment that employees find motivating.

Motivation is a set of factors that influence an individual's actions toward accomplishing a goal. Employees may be motivated to achieve company goals or they may be motivated to spend time in unproductive ways or on their own personal needs.

A manager makes a mistake by believing that all people are motivated by money or that all employees want the same things. There are many things in addition to salary and benefits that people find motivating about work. People value things like praise, respect, an interesting job assignment, or participating in an informal celebration with coworkers when a particularly challenging job is finished.

Motivation comes from both internal and external influences. *Internal motivation* results from strongly held beliefs and attitudes that affect a person's actions. For example, many people are motivated to attempt a new assignment because they like a challenge and want to be the first to try something.

Brainstorm with your classmates a list of internal motivators and another list of external motivators. Agree on the top ten items in each list. Using both lists, each student should select the three items that are personally the most effective motivators. Discuss similarities and differences among the choices.

External motivation comes from a person's response to rewards or punishments given by other people. If an employee does a particularly good job of completing an assignment, it may result in positive words from a manager, a customer, or coworker. A person may work hard to exceed the goals that have been set in the hope of receiving a bonus, a pay increase, or a promotion.

For some people internal factors have the most influence on their behavior. A person who is easily bored may have a difficult time completing a long work assignment well. Other people are motivated more by external factors. An employee may be motivated to work harder in order to be named "employee of the month" in the company newsletter. Accepting an employee's suggestion to change the way an activity is completed may increase the person's motivation.

All people have their own needs and will choose to do things that will satisfy those needs and avoid doing things that don't. Managers can influence employee performance by understanding individual needs and finding ways to satisfy those needs whenever possible.

CHECKPOINT

How can managers use the work environment and motivation to improve employee performance?

_____

_____

IMPROVE EMPLOYEE PERFORMANCE

In today's competitive environment, employee performance is more important than ever. Employees need to be able to do their work well and constantly find ways to improve the way work is done.

PERFORMANCE REVIEW PROCEDURES

Companies must make sure employees are performing as well as they possibly can. A **performance review** is the process of assessing how well employees are doing their jobs. The goal should be to recognize effective performance and make improvements where needed.

Companies use the information obtained from performance reviews for making new job assignments, offering salary increases, and providing training. All employees, including managers, should have a regular performance review. Many companies complete a formal review every six months.

The first step in developing a performance review process is to prepare the review form and procedures. Those forms and procedures should be designed to make the review process easy, understandable, and objective.

Each employee's review is based on the person's job duties and expectations. The manager completes the form after carefully observing the employee and reviewing his or her achievements. The employee may also complete a self-evaluation. The manager and employee then meet to discuss the results.

UNDERSTAND CULTURAL DIFFERENCES

Managers working with employees from other cultures must be particularly aware of differences in the way people work, communicate, and interact. Those differences will affect the way that positive work relationships develop and how managers can help employees be successful in their work.

For example, there are important cultural differences in how formal or informal a manager should be with an employee, the way criticism is given and received, and how a person asks for help or communicates understanding. Beliefs about gender roles may affect the way a female manager interacts with a male employee. Competition is an important motivator in some cultures while in others, people avoid appearing as if they are "better" than their coworkers.

THINK CRITICALLY What would you do to prepare if you were about to become the manager of a group of employees from several countries?

CONDUCT A PERFORMANCE REVIEW DISCUSSION

Performance review discussions are often a source of anxiety for both managers and employees. However, if carefully planned, the meeting should be a positive experience. The following suggestions help achieve that goal.

■ Schedule enough time for the discussion. Both people should plan for it by reviewing job duties, requirements, and the performance review form.

■ Have a discussion in which both people participate. The manager should not do all of the talking and the employee all of the listening.

■ Focus the discussion on the employee's performance, not on personal traits and character. Feedback should be based on objective information.

■ Show how the employee's work has contributed to the company's goals. Make sure the employee feels that his or her efforts are valued.

■ Discuss specific accomplishments and strengths. Identify any rewards or recognition the employee will receive.

■ Agree on areas that need improvement. Plan specific ways the employee can develop needed skills and improve performance and how the manager will support the improvement plan.

CHECKPOINT

What is the first step in developing a performance review procedure?

_____

_____

THINK CRITICALLY

1. Do you think most people are motivated to work effectively for their employer? Why or why not?

_____

_____

2. Should managers regularly use punishments for poor performance? Justify your answer.

_____

_____

_____

_____

3. Why do many employees and managers have a negative view of performance reviews?

_____

_____

_____

4. Do you think employees should have the opportunity to complete a performance review of their manager? Why or why not?

_____

_____

_____

MAKE CONNECTIONS

5. **PSYCHOLOGY** One of the most widely used theories of motivation is Maslow's Hierarchy of Needs. Gather information on Maslow's theory and prepare a chart that illustrates the 5 levels of need identified by Maslow. Describe a way that a business could respond to employee needs at each of the five levels. Present your chart in class.

_____

_____

_____

_____

6. **DESIGN** Locate an office area that is used by someone as his or her regular work area. The office can be in your school, in a business, or a home office. Obtain permission from the user of the work area to conduct a thorough analysis. Take a picture or sketch the office space, making sure to show the location of all furniture and equipment. Review the space, paying attention to how work is done. Prepare a set of recommendations on how the work space could be reorganized to improve the efficiency of the work and the comfort of the employee resulting in a more effective and motivating work environment.

LESSON 6.4
TRAIN AND DEVELOP

THE IMPORTANCE OF TRAINING

"If your business is not changing, you are falling behind." That well-known statement suggests that in today's global, competitive business environment, even the most successful companies cannot be content with business as usual. They must constantly look for new products, new customers, and ways to improve their operations and profits.

Individual employees need to heed the same advice. If you aren't finding ways to improve your knowledge and skills, you are not going to be as effective in your work. Education and training are essential for success in business. The companies that invest in employee training and development and the individuals who are continually improving their skills will be the leaders in the world marketplace.

ON THE $CENE

For the past two years since graduating from high school, Petrie has worked as a technician for the Celtron Company. He enjoys the work but knows it doesn't pay enough now that he and his fiancée are planning their wedding. He expects he will need additional education and training to move to the higher-paying positions and has even wondered what it would take to become a manager. He can see himself spending many years at Celtron but is uncertain of what steps to take to plan his career. What resources are available to help people like Petrie make career plans? How can Petrie determine the amount and type of education he will need for future jobs?

INVEST IN TRAINING

Training is a planned program to develop the skills needed by employees to perform a specific job. Businesses spend a great deal of money planning and delivering training to improve the productivity of their employees. It is estimated that U.S. companies spend between 50 and 60 billion dollars each year on formal training programs. Informal training (learning on the job, self study, coaching) may cost businesses as much as an additional $150 billion each year. On average, companies spend several hundred dollars on every employee each year for training.

Beyond the costs of training, some companies pay a part or all of the costs of college courses that employees complete. Many businesses sponsor basic education classes to improve reading and math skills for employees who may not have completed a high school education. The large amount of money for training and education can be justified if the spending results in employees who are able to perform more and higher quality work.

DETERMINE TRAINING NEEDS

An important activity for all companies is determining the need for employee training. Some training needs are quite obvious. All new employees need an orientation to the company and their job. Most also need some additional training on equipment and procedures to perform the job effectively.

When experienced employees are promoted to new jobs, they will usually not have all of the skills needed. If the company buys new equipment, begins new operations, or introduces improved procedures, managers and employees will need to be trained for the changes. Each of these situations is an obvious time for training.

Other training needs are not as obvious. Sometimes an employee performance review will identify problems in work performance. If a manager observes a work group with communication problems, records an increasing number of product defects, or begins to receive customer complaints, it may signal the need for training. Companies need to collect information to identify problems and determine whether training can help solve them. An ignored problem will not disappear.

COMPUTER-BASED TRAINING An increasingly popular method of training is computer-based training, where training is delivered to each employee using a computer and a carefully prepared training program. Employees can complete training at any time wherever they have access to a computer. They can spend as little or as much time as needed. The use of computers allows trainees to learn by reading, hearing, and watching. They view videos of correct procedures, take tests to determine if they have learned, and get additional training if needed. Computer-based training is frequently available through the Internet.

THINK CRITICALLY What advantages do you think computer-based training has over classroom training or on-the-job training? What disadvantages might it have?

CHAPTER 6

REVIEW CONCEPTS

10. What are the results of the work of people in the human resources department?

_____

_____

11. What are some things in addition to salary and benefits that satisfy employees?

_____

_____

_____

12. Identify several sources companies use to recruit new employees.

_____

_____

_____

13. Who should be involved in interviewing applicants for a new job?

_____

_____

_____

_____

14. What is the difference between external and internal motivation?

_____

_____

_____

_____

15. Who should complete the performance review form when an employee's work is being reviewed?

_____

_____

_____

_____

16. What is a career center?

_____

_____

_____

POINT YOUR BROWSER

b2000.swep.com

155

APPLY WHAT YOU LEARNED

17. Why is the human resources department more important to businesses today than in the past?

_____

_____

_____

_____

_____

18. What is the relationship between recruitment and selection of new employees and the training programs offered by a company?

_____

_____

_____

_____

_____

19. How can the use of employee teams contribute to job enrichment?

_____

_____

_____

_____

_____

20. What role should a manager play in the career development of an employee?

_____

_____

_____

_____

_____

_____

MAKE CONNECTIONS

21. SOCIOLOGY Locate and read newspaper and magazine articles on similarities and differences among employees in different age groups: under 30; 30–50; over 50. Find information on their feelings about jobs and careers. Write a one-page report on those differences and what a business needs to do to meet the needs of employees from each group.

22. DECISION MAKING When reviewing the applications of prospective employees, managers look for the right combination of education, experience, and specific knowledge and skill. For each of the following jobs, rank those three factors from most to least important in selecting the best person for the job. Write a brief rationale for each set of decisions. Then present your findings in class.

a. manager of a small retail business

_____
_____

b. web page designer

_____
_____
_____

c. physician's assistant

_____
_____
_____

23. CULTURE Use the Internet to gather information about another culture that would help you if you were the manager of an employee from that culture. Develop a written report on your findings and share the information with your classmate.

_____
_____
_____
_____

24. TECHNOLOGY One of the most effective training techniques is the use of computer simulations. In the simulation, a computer is used to present situations to the trainee using video images and sound that allow practice of the knowledge and skills needed on the job. Many current computer games sold to consumers present simulations of skills that are actually used on jobs. Visit a computer software store or search the Internet to identify examples of those computer games. Using a spreadsheet format, make a list of realistic training simulations you locate, the types of skills that are developed, and a job related to the simulation.

_____
_____
_____
_____

GLOSSARY

A

Authority employee's power to make decisions needed to complete the work without having to check with the manager (p. 33)

B

Banks financial institutions regulated by state or federal governments that offer loan and deposit services for individuals and businesses (p. 116)

Budget a specific, written financial plan (p. 121)

Business ethics principles of conduct guiding the actions of businesspeople (p. 21)

Business plan a written description of the business and its operations with an analysis of its strengths and the risks it faces (p. 11)

C

Capital the financial resources used to operate a business (p. 108)

Career development program a plan for meeting the company's future employment needs by systematically preparing current employees for future positions in the company (p. 151)

Career path a progression of related jobs with increasing skill requirements and responsibility (p. 152)

Charter legal document issued by a state granting the business the power to organize, issue stock, and complete specific activities (p. 10)

Communication the exchange of information between two or more people in a way that results in common understanding (p. 58)

Competition economic situation in which many businesses offer very similar products and services for sale (p. 5)

Consumer research gathering information about the experience and opinions of prospective customers (p. 88)

Consumers purchasers and users of the products and services produced by business (p. 5)

Controlling evaluating results to determine if the company's objectives have been accomplished as planned (p. 31)

Corporation form of business ownership in which a number of people own the business through the purchase of stock but have limited responsibility and liability (p. 10)

Creditworthiness a person's capability to pay for credit (p. 124)

D

Debt capital money obtained from sources other than business owners (p. 108)

Demand deposit money that can be withdrawn at any time with no financial penalty (p. 114)

E

Entrepreneur a person who takes the risk of starting and operating a business with the goal of making a profit (p. 9)

Environmental responsibility the duty of a business to protect the natural resources affected by its products and operations (p. 6)

Equity capital financial resources the owners of a business provide (p. 108)

Ethics the principles, beliefs, and values accepted by a society or culture that guide the conduct of individuals and groups (p. 21)

Executive top-level manager who spends most of his or her time on management functions (p. 32)

Exports products sold to customers in another country (p. 16)

F

Financial records organized summaries of a business's financial activities (p. 118)

H

Human relations refers to how well people get along with each other when working together (p. 36)

Human resources management (HRM) all of the activities involved with hiring, training, and compensating the people who work for a company (p. 134)

I

Implementing carrying out the plans and helping employees to work effectively (p. 31)

Imports products that are purchased from another country (p. 16)

Information management system a comprehensive process for obtaining, organizing, storing, and providing information to improve decision-making in an organization (p. 73)

Insurance limits the amount of financial loss from an uncontrollable event in exchange for a regular payment of money (p. 125)

International business any business activities that occur between two or more countries (p. 15)

J

Job description a list of the basic tasks that make up a job (p. 140)

Job design the kinds of tasks that make up a job and the way workers perform these tasks in doing their jobs (p. 145)

Job enrichment giving employees the authority to make meaningful decisions about their work (p. 145)

Job specification a list of the qualifications a worker needs to do that job (p. 140)

K

Knowledge workers people whose jobs require them to regularly access and use information (p. 74)

L

Leadership the ability to influence individuals and groups to cooperatively achieve organizational goals (p. 36)

Loan money borrowed for a specific period of time on which interest must be paid (p. 114)

M

Management the process of accomplishing the goals of an organization through the effective use of people and other resources (p. 30)

Management information the organized information and reports reviewed by managers and others to aid decision making (p. 73)

Manager a person who assumes responsibility for the successful operation of a business (p. 9)

Manufacturing a form of production in which raw and semifinished materials are processed, assembled, or converted into finished products (p. 83)

Marketing creating, distributing, pricing, and promoting products and services to meet customer needs at a profit (p. 92)

Marketing concept the needs of the consumer are considered during the design, production, and distribution of a product (p. 93)

Marketing mix the blending of all decisions related to the four elements of marketing-product, price, place, and promotion (p. 94)

Marketing strategy all of the important decisions made to successfully market a product or service (p. 93)

Media the methods used to move information between senders and receivers (p. 59)

Meetings situation involving small numbers of people who come together to address specific business issues (p. 66)

Middle manager responsible for a specific part of the company's operations such as sales or information management (p. 32)

Monopoly only one company provides a product or service without competition from other companies (p. 20)

Motivation a set of factors that influence an individual's actions toward accomplishing a goal (p. 145)

O

Operation plans specific plans that set direction for one part of the business for a short period of time (p. 41)

Operations the major ongoing activities of a business (p. 46)

Oral communication spoken words, body language, and listening used to convey information (p. 64)

Organization chart a visual device that shows the structure of the organization, the division of work, and the relationships among employees (p. 13)

Organizing determining how plans can be accomplished most effectively and arranging resources to complete work (p. 31)

P

Partnership form of business ownership in which two or more people own the business and share the risks, rewards, and responsibility for operations (p. 10)

Performance review the process of assessing how well employees are doing their jobs (p. 146)

Planning analyzing information and making decisions about what needs to be done (p. 31)

Process improvement efforts to increase the effectiveness and efficiency of specific business operations (p. 47)

Product all attributes, both tangible and intangible, that customers receive in exchange for the purchase price (p. 97)

Production all of the activities involved in creating products for sale (p. 83)

Product research research completed by engineers and other scientists to develop new products or to discover improvements for existing products (p. 88)

Proprietorship form of business ownership in which one person owns a business and takes the major responsibility for decisions about its operation (p. 10)

Q

Quality management a process for assuring product quality by developing standards for all operations and products and measuring results against those standards (p. 84)

R

Receiver one or more people with whom the sender wants to communicate (p. 59)

S

Sender the person or organization providing the information (p. 59)

Services activities of value that do not result in the ownership of anything tangible (p. 84)

Social responsibility the duty of a business to contribute to the well-being of society (p. 6)

Span of control the number of employees who report to one manager (p. 32)

Strategic plans broad and general plans that set direction for the entire business for a long period of time (p. 40)

Supervisor first level of management in a company whose main job is to direct the work of employees (p. 32)

Supply and demand economic principle that describes the relationship between production and consumption (p. 5)

T

Target market a group of customers that has very similar needs, and to whom the company plans to sell its product (p. 93)

Technology the practical application of science and engineering (p. 71)

Training a planned program to develop the skills needed by employees to perform a specific job (p. 150)

U

Unity of command management principle that each employee should have only one manager (p. 33)

W

Written communication text and images used to convey information (p. 64)

INDEX

PHOTO CREDITS

Cover art © EyeWire.
All photos © PhotoDisc, Inc.